WORDS OF WISDOM
FOR LIVING LIFE

A Book of Philosophical Thoughts on Life

"TREE OF LIFE" ©
Cover Design By: Tony Yep

A WHITE TREE AGAINST A BLACK BACKGROUND
TO REPRESENT LIFE AND DEATH

White "Tree of Life" represents the search
for knowledge and enlightenment.

Black represents the unknowns of Death
and the dark emptiness of the Universe.

This image shows the reverse of black and
white when enlightenment is attained.

Then the darkness of Death is no longer
an unsolved mystery of Life.

WORDS OF WISDOM
FOR LIVING LIFE

A Book of Philosophical Thoughts on Life

TONY YEP

ISBN 978-1-7771212-2-8 Hardcover Version
ISBN 978-1-7771212-0-4 Paperback Version
ISBN 978-1-7771212-1-1 Electronic Book

Library and Archives Canada Cataloguing in Publication and Library of Congress Cataloging Number (LCCN)
Pending on Hardcover Version

First Edition 2020

DEDICATION

I wrote this book for my grandchildren – Kyle, Evan, Gwen and Nathan – who one day may seek answers to these existential questions on Life. Then they will realize that Yeh-Yeh, their grandfather, had been thinking of them all along.

ACKNOWLEDGEMENTS

I would like to acknowledge the following people who helped me make this book my "once in a lifetime" endeavour.

K. Houlgate (www.guildstreet.ca) for her excellent feedback and editing support.

Richard Bloemhof for our many philosophical discussions on science and religion.

Nattalia Lea, author of "Lady with the Iron Ring", for her informative workshop on how to publish books.

Special thanks to **Mary O'Neil** and my brother-in-law, **Steve Roper** (www.steveroper.life), whose ideas and opinions I have always respected. Their feedback and comments were invaluable.

Final acknowledgement and appreciation to my wife, **Patricia**, who has always been there for me.

TABLE OF CONTENTS

Section I:
Examinations of Life's
Existential Questions

Section II:
My Conclusions on Fate,
Death and the Meaning of life

Section III:
Words of Wisdom (WOW)
Quotations for Living Life

PREFACE

Life has always been a struggle for many and evil has always existed. There are unknown forces of creation much greater than we can imagine that govern all things in the Universe. Some call this God, or the forces of Nature. Either can be true as neither can be proven or disproven. Our impact to the Universe is truly insignificant. All the accumulated knowledge, power, wealth and prestige that we have acquired during our lifetime and the great civilizations we have built will eventually die and disappear into nothingness, given enough time. That is Life. Relentless time and the ever-changing Universe will render anything we do meaningless.

That is the message of the poem:

OZYMANDIAS – By Percy Bysshe Shelley (1792-1822)

I met a traveler from an antique land
Who said: Two vast and trunkless legs of stone
Stand in the desert. Near them, on the sand,
Half sunk, a shattered visage lies, whose frown,
And wrinkled lip, and sneer of cold command.
Tell that its sculptor well those passions read
Which yet survive, stamped on these lifeless things,
The hand that mocked them and the heart that fed;
And on the pedestal these words appear:
"My name is Ozymandias, king of kings:
Look on my works, ye Mighty, and despair!"
Nothing beside remains. Round the decay
Of that colossal wreck, boundless and bare
The lone and level sands stretch far away.

Why do we continue to exist, when our lives have seemingly no real relevancy or purpose? This book strives to provide answers that are reasonable and logical, based on the things you may have already seen, experienced, or thought of. Despite this rather harsh view of life that nothing is permanent, in our world of opposites, life can be looked at optimistically, that it does matter to us individually, and that life is worth living, for however long or short it may be.

People, from ancient times to the present, have contemplated what this life of ours is all about. They searched for answers to the purpose and meaning of life. Many of their recorded quotations reflect some simple truths in life that are familiar to us. This book has compiled some of the best of these quotations on life. These "words of wisdom" come from the great philosophers and scientists, from the powerful and the rich and famous, and from the poor and struggling people. These quotations provide insights why life continues to be the way it is and what things are needed to find meaning and fulfilment in your own life.

A BOOK OF PHILOSOPHICAL
THOUGHTS ON LIFE

PROLOGUE

This is the first book I have written. It is not the first time I have ever written anything for publication. As an engineer, I have written many technical papers and reports, but these were always factual, to the point and rather dry. To make my book engaging and not telling you what to do, but letting you draw your own conclusions, were definite challenges for me. I am so used to telling people directly what to do. The subject matter is also very difficult and profound. Heavy stuff! But it was something I had to do as it has taken me this long just to acquire the life experience needed to be able to write a book that would not only be easy to understand, but hopefully also useful and meaningful to you. I tried my best to be "engaging". You can be the judge of that.

This book has three Sections:

Section I – "Examinations of Life's Existential Questions"

This Section identifies the issues of Life as pieces of a puzzle which are to be put together to see the "big picture" of why Life is the way it is. Each chapter is a piece of the puzzle representing some aspect of Life, and it attempts to provide the information necessary to better understand the context of the existential questions. These insights are done from a philosophical perspective to show that the philosophers throughout recorded history have pondered these same questions that we are still seeking answers to. You may have experienced many of these insights, but you may not have thought about them in the way they are presented here. Hopefully at the end, after you have read all the chapters and got all the pieces, you will be able to complete this puzzle of life and have a better understanding of who you are and what your life means to you.

Section II - "My Conclusions About Fate, Death and the Meaning of Life"

This next Section takes all the knowledge from the initial section and integrates these thoughts in defining my conclusions about fate, death and the meaning of life. No doubt, you will be drawing your own conclusions as to the purpose and meaning of your life.

Section III – "Quotations for Living Life"

This final Section is a summary compilation of all the quotations used in this book. There are over 250 quotations that reflect some aspects of life. These quotes may be philosophical and profound, or offering sage advice on how to live a better life, or be downright whimsical and silly, showing how capricious life can be. It is hoped that many of these quotes will resonate personally with you.

Let us start. I invite you to join me on this journey of discovery into the mysteries of our existence. See, I have started to be engaging!

SECTION I
EXAMINATIONS OF LIFE'S EXISTENTIAL QUESTIONS

Chapter 1

INTRODUCTION

H ave you ever thought "Why things are the way they are in life?" Well, you are not alone thinking this. For the past 3000 years, great philosophers have pondered these universal questions:

- "Who are we?"
- "Where does the world come from?"
- "Is there a God?"
- "Is life an illusion?"
- "Is there life after death?"
- "What is the meaning of life?"
- "Where does evil come from?"
- "Why are men and women so different?"

These questions remain unanswered and they are still relevant in our time. This book presents thoughts and perspectives on life that may provide new insights into why life is as it is and whether there is any meaning and purpose to our existence.

In ancient times, before the advent of any of the world's great religions, people were already questioning the existence of God and why there is evil in the world. This is demonstrated by the quote:

Epicurus (341-270 BC)
"Is God willing to prevent evil, but not able? Then he is not omnipotent. Is he able, but not willing? Then he is malevolent. Is he both able and willing? Then whence cometh evil? Is he neither able nor willing? Then why call him God?"

Human reasoning and all our knowledge acquired over the centuries remain inadequate in either proving or disproving the existence of God. In such cases where no logical or proven explanation exists, we must rely on faith, or our religion, to believe that there has to be a Creator somewhere and that our existence has to have some meaning and purpose. Every one of us needs to believe in something to live and to survive.

Every individual is unique. There is just a single one of each of us who will only live once. Even identical twins will have differences. What you believe is influenced by your race, gender, culture, upbringing, education and environment.

Which of the following best reflect who you are and the beliefs that you hold to be true to you? There is no right or wrong in what you choose. It just reflects what your beliefs are at this phase of your life.

- <u>Deist</u>: A person who believes that God created the world ages ago, and has not revealed himself or herself to the world since. Thus, God is reduced to the "Supreme Being" who is only revealed to humankind through nature and natural laws, and never in any "supernatural" way.

- <u>Pantheist</u>: A person who believes that God is infinite and present everywhere in the creation of all things and the Universe.

- <u>Creationist</u>: A person who believes that the true story of the creation of the Universe and all things is recounted in the Bible.

- <u>Polytheist</u>: A person who believes in many gods, as in Hinduism. There are those who believe in a feminine god.

- <u>Monotheist</u>: A person who believes in only one God, as in Christianity, Judaism and Islam.

- <u>Agnostic:</u> A person who holds that the existence of God or a god can neither be proved nor disproved.

- <u>Atheist</u>: A person who denies or disbelieves the existence of any supreme being or beings.

- <u>Fatalist</u>: A person who believes in Determinism that everything that happens is pre-determined. "It is written in the stars that something will happen."

- <u>Nihilist</u>: A person who thinks nothing means anything and everything is permissible. In other words, "nothing matters."

- <u>Realist</u>: A person who tends to view or represent things as they really are. This is the opposite of an idealist. Trouble with either is whether their respective perception of reality is the right one.

- <u>Idealist:</u> A person who represents things as they might or should be, rather than as they are.

- <u>Existentialist:</u> A person who believes in the individual's importance as the only self-determining entity responsible for his or her own choices, that we are in control of our own destiny.

- <u>Scientist:</u> A person who believes that the principles and methods of the physical and biological sciences will provide the knowledge to better understand life and the workings of the Universe.

In this context, what are you? What or who do you believe in? At the end of this section, I will tell you what I believe to be true.

<u>My Viewpoint:</u>
Everyone will have different beliefs and opinions on these existential questions. That is the world we live in. There is no right or wrong in what you believe to be true. ***This is what makes you who you are. Everyone is unique and your life is special to you.***

Chapter 2

IS THERE A GOD?

Is there a God that created all life and the Universe? The early Greek philosophers tried to find natural, rather than supernatural, explanations for causes like creation and the way the world was perceived. Then religious doctrines and faith were introduced to explain the unknowns when reasoning alone was not sufficient. Later philosophers raised further thoughts to the eternal questions as new truths and scientific knowledge became apparent.

The creation of life and the Universe has been questioned since the history of humanity's recorded time as demonstrated by the following quotes:

Democritus (460-370 BC)
"Nothing can come from nothing. Nothing can change, and nothing is lost."

Rumi (1207-1273)
"We come whirling out of nothingness, scattering stars like dust."

Rene Descartes (1596-1650) believed that the idea of God was innate in everyone, that it was a logical and rational conclusion. God had to exist as the idea of such a perfect entity, as the source of all creation, could not have originated from an imperfect thing like a human being. It must have been there from the very beginning. Trouble with this reasoning is that if God created the Universe, then who created God?

With regard to whether there is, or is not, the existence of a God, most people will agree that human reasoning is not capable of either proving or disproving it. We can either believe it, or we don't. Yet it is difficult to see how nature and the Universe could have been conceived without some intelligence behind it. When one looks at the wonders of the Universe in its organized chaos of stars and galaxies and the complex intricacies of life that can produce the simple beauty of a fluttering butterfly or the fragrant scent of a flower, one can only marvel at creation and conclude that something had to have created all this. We can see that creation could not have come from nothing.

Carl Sagan (1934-1996)
"A Universe with no edge in space, no beginning or end in time, and nothing for a Creator to do."

Depending on what you believe God to be, the answer to this question may be a profound truth, as defined by the following quote:

Niels Bohr (1855-1962)
"There are two kinds of truths. There are the superficial truths, the opposite of which are obviously wrong. But there are also the profound truths, whose opposites are equally right".

An example of a superficial truth would be: the male species originated from the basic female form whereas the opposite would say, according to the Bible, that the first female, Eve, was created from Adam's rib. In other words, the female form came from a male. This latter case is obviously wrong when viewed with the biological science and human anatomy we know today. When asked the simple question, "Why do men have nipples?", it becomes obvious that men have no need for nipples and that men must have evolved from the basic female form which is the dominant form for all living animal life. A profound truth would be that men and women were derived from a natural evolutionary process following the laws of nature. The opposite of this would be that men and women were created by God, or a supernatural process. Both are correct even if you don't believe there is such a God. The laws of nature had to be created by something. They could not have come from nothing. So who created these laws of nature?

The point here is that no matter what or who you believe to be the originator of creation, we all need to believe in something that is true to us, something that would give us the peace of mind to continue living despite not knowing how we were created.

My Viewpoint:
Science has not been able to either prove or disprove the existence of a God, or gods, or some supreme force of creation. Whatever you believe will always be subjective and personal to you. This question **whether there is or is not a God is a profound truth, as both can be correct for you.**

Chapter 3

FAITH VERSUS REASON

Throughout history, religions have played important roles in offering possible answers to the universal questions of life, especially when reason and logic alone were not sufficient to explain the mysteries of creation and the Universe. Religions continue to be relevant. There is so much we still do not know and will probably never know. Faith through religion must fill the gaps in our knowledge, when logic and reasoning fail. What religious truths we believe in may not be reasonable, or even possible. They only have to be true to us.

The great Western religions of Christianity, Judaism and Islam all share the same fundamental idea that there is only one God. In the beginning, God created humankind and the Universe, and at the end on Judgment Day, God will judge the living and the dead. The purpose of life was to be redeemed from sin through salvation. This meant living a moral life through prayer and good deeds, sermons and study of the scriptures. In Christianity, man's disobedience to God is a theme prevalent in the Bible, and the reason why death and the concept of heaven and hell came into our world. Through faith in Jesus Christ, everyone can be saved from death and "damnation."

In the Eastern religions like Hinduism and Buddhism, they emphasize the fusion with a God being a cosmic spirit which could be manifested by many gods. This deity, or cosmic spirit, is present in all things (pantheism) and humans can become one with God through the religious insights achieved through deep self-communion or meditation. The principal aim of Buddhist psychology is fundamentally to overcome suffering by clearing out psychological and emotional affliction. The key afflictions are seen to be expressions of attachment (materialism), anger and delusion.

All the great religions in the world promote the tenets of living a moral and ethical life filled with compassion and tolerance, kindness and love for self, and forgiveness and caring for fellow humans. They offered "rules" for attaining happiness through a life doing good deeds by not killing, stealing, lying or exploiting others for one's personal gain, by not being selfish and self-centered and to not be overly attached to the pursuit of material things. Living a moral life meant being truthful and honest and being a person with integrity, good thoughts and intents devoid of sexual misconduct and desires. Only then will you be rewarded in a better life after death. All human beings are the same in their search for happiness and relief from suffering. Even people who do not believe in religion recognize these human values can only make their lives, and those around them, better.

There are many who believe that all religions and their "rules" are human-made. After all, if there is a God, he certainly does not need a set of rules to show his creations what they needed to do to reach salvation and be rewarded with a better life after death. Yet people persist in relying on their religions to provide them guidance and structure in how they should live their life, and the solace in knowing their fate after death.

Some philosophers had a harsh view of any organized religion, that they are like drugs, skewing reality and controlling the thoughts and actions of people:

Karl Marx (1818-1883)
"Religion is the sigh of the oppressed creature … the heart of a heartless world, and the soul of the soul-less conditions. It is the opium of the people."

Other philosophers take a more inclusive and positive view of the important role religions play in providing comfort and structure in our world of unknowns:

Dalai Lama (1935-Present)
"Promotion of religious harmony is needed to understand the different religious traditions. Despite the philosophical differences, all the major world religions have the same potential to create better human beings. It is important for all religions to respect one another and to recognize the value of each other's respective traditions."

Whether you view your faith and your religion positively or negatively depends on what beliefs you hold to be true. Your beliefs are distinctly personal and there is no right or wrong in this matter. Your beliefs make you who you are.

FAITH VERSUS REASON

My Viewpoint:

Reason and science can only go so far in explaining the workings of life and the Universe. Where they are inadequate or incomplete, faith and religion must fill the gaps to make sense of the reality each of us hold to be true. **Religions, throughout history, have played important roles influencing the lives of all human beings, for better or for worse.**

CHAPTER 4

WHAT IS LIFE?

In Christianity, life is a constant struggle for survival between good and evil, and it has always been filled with suffering. In Buddhism, life is seen as an unbroken succession of mental and physical processes and struggles which keep people in a continual state of change. Suffering is present when we get sick and our health fails, or when people we care for and love die for one reason or another, or when we are oppressed and taken advantage of by others, and when we die unexpectedly before it is our time. This is a rather pessimistic view of life considering that life can also be filled with much joy, wonder and happiness.

In ancient times, life was indeed harsh. It was a daily physical struggle just to get enough food and shelter to survive and the lifespan was much shorter back then. There was much suffering from diseases and poor hygiene. They did not have the benefits of the modern medicine as we have today. The living conditions were less than optimal not having the technological and engineering conveniences and comforts of our modern civilizations. Suffering still exists today. We continue to have diseases and poverty, corruption and immoral individuals and leaders of countries seeking power and material wealth, oppressing the people in the process.

For many, daily life can be a harsh reality that promotes and prolongs suffering, especially if there is nothing to live for. Everyone has experienced some aspects of suffering in life.

Leonard Cohen (1934-2016)
From his song: Everybody Knows - *"... that the dice are loaded ... that the war is over and the good guys lost ... that the boat is leaking and the captain lied ... that the fight was fixed, and the poor stay poor and the rich get rich."*

Life exists for plants, animals and humans. Biological science has confirmed that life started from single celled micro-organisms which could sense and react to their environment. Eventually with time, these micro-organisms and cells evolved to become species of plants and animals and humans we know today. All living things interact with the environment they are exposed to. Animals and humans became sentient, being conscious of their surroundings. In the case of humans, we are the only species that can drastically alter our environment to suit our needs. Strangely, all living things need to sleep. Why do we need to sleep and lose so much of our limited life just sleeping? And why do humans, in particular, dream when we sleep? Dreams that can be so vivid, that they blur our sense of reality. And where did our consciousness and conscience come from? These are just other unsolved mysteries of life.

Life is the luck of the draw whether you are born as a male or female. It is what it is and you have no choice in this matter. If you are fortunate enough to be born into a wealthy family of nobility where all your physical and financial needs are taken care of, then you will suffer less and have a life of comfort and leisure. If you end up being born to a poor family, living in poverty and squalor, your life will be much harder with more obstacles and hardships just to survive your daily existence. Whoever you are, it will be your life to live.

Life is short and fleeting. When you die, whoever you are and whatever you did during your lifetime and the legacies you left behind, they will all disappear in time and be forgotten – like what the poet Shelley said in his poem "Ozymandias". In the context of the Universe, it doesn't matter whether you are rich and powerful, or famous, or poor and ordinary, your life becomes irrelevant at death. In my youth, this famous quote from Shakespeare on life didn't resonate with me as I was too immersed in my daily struggles to make a career of my life and to care for my family .... to just survive. I had little time to think about life. Now with the wisdom and experience attained with age, I now understand and appreciate how truly insignificant my life really is.

William Shakespeare (1564-1616)
From Macbeth: *"Life is but a walking shadow, a poor player that struts and frets his hour upon the stage and then is heard no more. It is a tale told by an idiot, full of sound and fury, signifying nothing."*

This simple quote puts into context that life should be the only thing meaningful to us. At the end, death is the common denominator for all living things.

Harlan Edison (1934-2018)
"For a brief time, I was here. And for a brief time, I mattered."

WHAT IS LIFE?

My Viewpoint:

*Life is special to you for however long or short you may live. You are a sentient being, gifted with a conscience and the intelligence to reason. You have some control in what you choose to do and how you intend to live your life. **Make the best of it. Your life is only yours to live**.*

Chapter 5

IS THERE LIFE AFTER DEATH?

This question is second to whether there is a God. To answer this, I have to tell you a story of the time I met a person who claimed to be a futurist, making a living doing so. A futurist is a person who claims to be able to predict what will happen in the future, somewhat akin to fortune tellers and tarot card or tea leaves readers. Strangely, many people truly believe in such mystic powers to predict the future, and they would willingly pay for such "advice". Horoscopes are regularly included in the newspapers. I told this individual that I do not believe in such things. As a trained engineer, I must rely on logical outcomes based on established and proven truths. I couldn't design and build things based on the unknown and the unproven. But I also told him that my mind was open as there are many things that cannot be explained through logic and reason. For example, there are people who are very adept at dowsing, that peculiar skill of finding water using a forked willow branch as a divining rod that "twitched" when close to a source of water. Or the people who claim to be able to "sense" unseen ghosts and para-normal events. Not everyone could do it, but maybe there are individuals who happen to be super-sensitive to the electro-magnetic waves all around us. So, I gave him the benefit of the doubt that maybe he was one of those gifted individuals with supernatural powers of perception.

Then he went one step further and said that "he could speak to the dead!" Now my logical brain would simply not accept that this was possible. So, I asked him, "When you were speaking to the dead, did you ever ask them what this white light was and where they are now?" I was trying to find out if there was indeed a heaven or hell, and whether God was that white light which those people who had died temporarily and recalled when they were resuscitated back to life. Not surprisingly, he didn't have an answer. But I didn't expect him to. There is no such supernatural power. If he had the answer to what was life after death, he would have been world famous as everyone would have wanted to know. So, the mystery remains unanswered.

If there is life after death, do we have a soul? In Christianity, everybody has a unique soul which is immortal and everlasting. Whether you ended up in heaven or hell depended on how well you lived your life and whether that was good enough for you to attain salvation and the promised everlasting life. Buddhism, however, does not believe in the immortality of the human soul, but it accepts that our existence will continue through reincarnation. This rebirth is not of the soul, but from body to body as one can be reborn as a god, or a different human, or an animal or as a suffering entity. Like Christianity, what good (karma) you have done during your life will determine what you will become in reincarnation.

David Hume (1711-1776) rejected any attempts to prove the immortality of the soul or the existence of God. But he didn't rule them out, as to prove religious faith by human reasoning was not rational. He didn't believe that there was life after death only because he hadn't experienced it, not because it might be possible. A dilemma persists when everything and anything cannot be proved or disproved, such as the existence of God or whether there is life after death.

Immanuel Kant (1724-1804) said that for questions where both reason and experience fall short, we must then rely on our faith, or what we believe to be true, to fill the gaps. It was also essential for our peace of mind to believe and accept that a human does have an immortal soul and that a God of some form must exist,

IS THERE LIFE AFTER DEATH?

even though they cannot be proven. This is another example of a profound truth. If you believe there is a God, then that is your reality.

My Viewpoint:
No one knows for sure whether there is some kind of life after death, or what will become of us. So why worry needlessly about the unknown future we have no control over. Whatever will be will be. **_We did not come from nothingness, and whatever our existence will be at death, it will be something!_** _Maybe something we least expect._

Chapter 6

IS LIFE AN ILLUSION?

There is an ancient quote which questions whether our reality is real, or is it just a dream.

Chuang Tzu (369-286 BC)
"Once I dreamed I was a butterfly, and now I no longer know whether I am I, who dreamed I was a butterfly, or whether I am a butterfly dreaming that I am I."

George Berkeley (1685-1753) believed that everything exists in God and he is the cause of everything that exists, and that we exist only in the mind of God. This aligns with Pantheism, the doctrine that God was infinite and present everywhere in creation and in all things: that God is the transcendent reality of which the material world and humanity are only manifestations. He argued that the physical world did not exist independently of how the mind perceives it. Things only existed when they are observed; otherwise, they are non-existent or meaningless. In other words, our reality may only be in our minds.

This thought was also raised by _Rene Descartes (1596-1650)_ who doubted everything, even what our senses tell us. _"How can you be certain that your whole life is not a dream?" He_ questioned how we can be assured that what we perceive with our reason really correspond to our reality. Many philosophers before him reached the end of the road at this very point. His famous quote: _"Cogito, ergo sum" or "I think, therefore I am",_ means our existence or our reality is what exists in our minds.

No one knows why we need to sleep and whether our dreams are any more "real" than our reality when we are awake. Dreams occur only when we sleep. Maybe our subconscious is trying to tell us something? _Sigmund Freud (1856-1939)_ said that all dreams are wish fulfilments, or a _"disguised fulfillment of a repressed wish."_ Maybe dreams are our wish for an alternate reality?

In Buddhism, the mind is the creator of the entire Universe. Other writers have made similar observations whether our reality exists only in our minds or in our dreams:

Novalis (1722-1801)
"The world becomes a dream, and the dream becomes reality".

Samuel Coleridge (1772-1834)
"What if you slept? And what if, in your sleep, you dreamed? And what if, in your dream, you went to heaven and there plucked a strange and beautiful flower? And what if, when you awoke, you had the flower in your hand? Ah, what then?"

We have all had dreams that we either remember vividly or vaguely when we awake. We've also had nightmares when something was chasing us, but never quite catching or killing us because we always managed to wake up before we were killed in our dreams. But what happens if we actually died in our dreams? Does this mean that we are also dead in real life? If yes, what then is really real?

There is a concept in Buddhism (3rd to 4th century) which describes the reality in an unusual way. It is called "emptiness", or the fundamental truth that "the way we perceive reality is not the way things really are". People believe that human beings have a unique existential status among living things because only humans possess some kind of "soul" or "self-consciousness". Our free will and mental capacity to reason and innovate give us the false belief that we can control our destiny and the environment we live in, that our reality is real to us. But from the Universe's perspective, humanity's existence and our accomplishments are "empty". Our reality is meaningless as it is not the reality of the Universe.

Our reality is based on what we perceive through our five basic senses of sight, touch, hearing, smell and taste – all which are manifested by tangible actions or materials that are governed by the immutable laws of causation. In other words, these sensations are the tangible results or products from a cause and effect process. Our sixth sense is the mental capacity such as thoughts and emotions, intention and conception, memories and recollections, perception and intuition, morality and ethics – all which do not produce any "real" and tangible outcomes since they reside in our minds. These thought processes include abstract thinking and dreams and our conscience. However, the mind decides what is real for us. The experience of consciousness is entirely subjective. Science has no definition of consciousness.

To be "full" or "not empty", all things and events, whether material or mental, must be devoid of any independent existence where the laws of cause and effect do not apply. There is nothing in our reality that is not a result of some cause and effect. There are very few things and events that are entirely self-contained and independent. The few examples which meet these criteria are the belief of a God, the workings of the Universe, and the concept of constant change with infinite time.

All of humankind's endeavors and material creations are subject to the laws of causation and their existence are not intrinsically independent. Our reality is "empty" from the perspective of the Universe. Our concerns about global warming, the rising sea levels due to the receding polar ice caps, world pollution and the degradation of our environment, and humankind's own self-destructive nature are only relevant to our perception of our reality and our expectations of what our world should be like. They mean absolutely nothing to the existence of the Universe. And the very short lifespan of human beings makes our existence even more insignificant. If the Universe wanted to wipe out mankind, it could easily do this by having a rogue asteroid the size of the moon strike the earth, or to release a natural plague which had no cure. Then the cycle of life can start all over again from scratch.

An analogy of this scenario would be the life cycle of the mayfly which is a mere 24 hours from birth to death. For us, the existence of the mayfly is meaningless. Whatever the mayfly did during its short life was "empty" in its impact to us. However, from the mayfly's perspective, this one day of life represented a whole lifetime, and it was everything to it. Our life is like this, too. Not only is our reality real to us, it is everything to us, no matter how long or short a life we may live. That is why life is so meaningful to us, despite being so insignificant to the Universe. This is the only reality we know and the only life we have. This may explain why humankind seems to be totally fixated on day-to-day issues of our lives even when we know that what we do will have no lasting impact whatsoever to the Universe. We cannot control the universal forces of nature and creation, so why spend time even thinking about the things we cannot do or understand! This just creates more existential angst. Better to concentrate our efforts and energies to issues in life that we think can control, even though our efforts may be futile and irrelevant from the Universe's perspective.

Quantum mechanics presents a mystery in life that remains unexplained. Its famous and puzzling double-slit experiment actually confirms this Buddhist concept of "emptiness", that the reality we perceive through our senses is not the reality that really exists. This experiment shoots electron particles one at a time at two vertical and parallel slits to a receptor plate which records where those particles that passed through the narrow slits had landed. Our reality, based on our senses, expects to see a dotted distribution pattern of two vertical lines mirroring the two vertical slits, which it does so repeatedly every time we observe the experiment. However, when we do not observe what is happening, the resulting pattern is not the two vertical lines expected, but a multitude of vertical lines more representative of a wave distribution as opposed to a particle. How can this be? How can a particle change to become a wave simply by not looking at it? Who is this observer? Is it us? How can an observer affect our reality? Our reality sees particles where the Universe's reality shows waves. Which one is real? Can it be that the reality we see is not the reality that truly exists? This is the very same definition of the Buddhist concept of "emptiness" postulated centuries ago! The unknown forces of creation surely have warped senses of humour to leave us with such an impossible and contrary conundrum to figure out - one that challenges our very sense of our reality.

Here is a simple example that might better explain this relative nature of reality and the role of the observer. When a tree falls in the forest and there is no one there to observe it, does it make a sound? If you say yes, then whose reality are you referring to? Who is the observer, the tree or you? It is definitely not the tree's reality as it has no ears to hear the sound. Its reality will be very different than your reality. Then the next question is which reality is real, and how do you know? Think of reality of the tree as being us, and then consider how different this reality would be if we were the Universe. Does this make more sense? Reality is subjective to the thing itself. Our reality is real to us because it is the only reality we know. But it may be a false reality not reflective of how things really are.

In the end, life may be an illusion, without any substance or reality, like the dream that will be forgotten upon awakening. It is possible that life exists only in our mind, or consciousness, and that it may indeed be a dream. Like the other philosophical questions, such a hypothesis can be a possibility of our reality, as it, too, cannot be proven nor disproven.

My Viewpoint:
From our perspective, the life we perceive through our senses and thoughts reflect the reality that is "real" to us. And throughout our life, we feel that we have some control over the things that affect our reality. However, from the Universe's perspective, our existence and our accomplishments are meaningless, or "empty". Given enough time, we will never have any lasting impact on the workings of the Universe. ***While meaningless to the Universe, our life means everything to us as this is the only reality that we know and the only life we have.***

Chapter 7

WHERE DID HUMANS COME FROM?

In ancient times, the philosophers had already thought about the creation of human beings. It is amazing to see how close they were to the origin of creation before the science of quantum mechanics or the biological theory of evolution were even discovered.

Parmenides (540-480 BC) believed in the existence of a single basic substance as the source of all things. We now know this substance to be atoms and other sub-atomic particles as defined in quantum mechanics.

Anaxagoras (500-428 BC) believed that nature is built up of an infinite number of minute particles invisible to the eye; and that everything can be divided into even smaller parts. These miniscule particles have "something of everything" in them – meaning the whole exists in each tiny part. We now know this to be the DNA in our cells.

The major breakthrough theory of gradual geological evolution came from *Sir Charles Lyell (1797 – 1875)* who stated that minute gradual changes over a long period of time could result in drastic alterations. This theory says that given enough time, many things in nature will evolve and change.

This caused *Friedrich Schelling (1775-1854)* to postulate the possible development in nature that something could evolve from earth to rock to the human mind. He believed in the gradual transitions from inanimate nature to more complicated life forms were possible. Nature was thought to be an organism constantly developing its innate potentialities. This was the first time it was thought that given sufficient time, life can evolve from lifeless things like rocks. Yet the facts revealed by the science of biological evolution are compelling. All living things continue to live, evolve and perish. This reality is all around us.

Then *Charles Darwin (1809-1882)* established the theory of organic evolution that all living things, including human beings, were the results of a slow biological evolution through the laws of nature and the process of natural selection. We now know that mutations over time in our DNA result in the variations in the species to continually improve their chances for survival through evolution and ongoing changes in nature and the environment. Darwin's theory of evolution, however, is deficient in explaining the origin of sentience, other than humans and animals have it.

This revolutionary theorem of natural organic evolution created quite an uproar in established religions like Christianity, which believed that God created humankind and all things. It was blasphemy to even consider that humans could have come from rocks!

Jean-Paul Sartre (1905-1980) said that existence does not mean the same as being alive. All living things have their own distinct characteristics and qualities. Plants and animals are alive. But humans are the only living creatures that are highly conscious of their own existence. And this existence takes priority over everything else. Humans have no innate "nature" of being something other than being human beings as dictated by our genes. Humans must create their own nature or essence, and what they do with their lives.

What humankind will evolve to is unknown as our evolution has not ended. We are unique in that we are capable of creating and building complex and amazing things; but we also have the ability to completely destroy ourselves and our environment. Not only are we adaptable to our surroundings, we can change our environment and living conditions to suit our needs. We can dominate and control all other living species. Our most distinguishable characteristic is our innate ability to reason, to seek the cause of the event, the "why." We have the mental capacity and consciousness to question the purpose of our existence. It is this reason why philosophers throughout the ages continue to search for answers to "why?" This has caused angst and anxiety when we try to answer questions that cannot be answered.

My Viewpoint:
*Through the biological sciences, it has been confirmed that human beings were created by the natural process of evolution that took thousands of years for humans to become what we are today. It is entirely possible, given enough time, that living organisms and life can evolve from inanimate things like rocks. **We are fortunate to be so unique amongst the living things on earth. We should be thankful that we are not rocks!***

Chapter 8

WHAT ARE THE LAWS OF NATURE?

The philosophers have long observed the workings of nature in searching for answers to the eternal question of who or what humankind is. _Antisthenes (455-360 BC)_ believed that nothing happens accidentally and that all living things followed some unbreakable laws of nature which govern all the natural processes, such as birth, sickness and death. _Aristotle (384-322 BC)_ believed that there is a purpose and a kind of "universal reasoning" guiding everything that happens in nature. _David Hume (1711-1776)_ postulated a "Law of Causation" which is the underpinning of the "laws of nature"- that everything that happens in nature must have both a cause and effect which are inherent to the thing itself. For example, if an animal is a herbivore, it will search for plants to satisfy its hunger.

If it is a hungry carnivore, it inherently knows as part of its nature not to eat plants, but other animals.

The laws of nature are neither good nor bad, reasonable nor unreasonable. They simply are what they have always been. There are two dominant laws of nature. The struggle for survival, including the biological imperative to reproduce, is the highest priority. This innate need to survive and to pro-create to prolong its species is hard-wired in the DNA of all living things. When animals are being hunted or threatened by a forest fire, they will run to escape death and to survive. The dandelion that is trying to eke out an existence in a harsh environment like a crack in the sidewalk will strive to flower early so its airborne seeds can be released in the wind to become dandelions elsewhere. No living things purposely kill themselves, except maybe humans (through suicides or medically assisted dying) when suffering becomes unbearable. Nature has its own way of keeping living things in balance by limiting the amount of food and habitat available to sustain life. Nature also has the ability to destroy all living things through natural disasters like rampant diseases, volcanic eruptions, earthquakes, lightning and fires, drought, tornadoes, hurricanes and floods.

One can say that this primary natural law of survival gives humans an innate and common purpose for living. Whether this purpose provides any satisfactory answer to the "meaning" of one's life will be very subjective to each individual. Are you happy just to be living your life solely to survive?

The second law of nature governs what each living thing must do to meet the first law of survival. This is the law of natural selection, or the survival of the fittest. Only the best specimens of each species will survive and be dominant – the strongest, fastest, smartest or most adaptable – and their traits will be passed onto further generations to ensure their continued existence. This law of natural selection is constantly evolving so that the species would become the one best suited for survival in any given environment. Humans have already tried to tamper with this natural selection process. We saw this in Hitler's experiments in trying to create an Aryan master race of super tall, fit and good-looking white Caucasians. We see this in the cloning of animals and in the human-made genetically modified plants made to be herbicide resistant to increase crop yields.

The natural evolutionary process will create mutations, or "super" forms with superior traits and survival mechanisms. If humans can control their self-destructive ways (nature's way of keeping humankind in check) and continue evolving in accordance with these laws of nature, a better species should evolve – one that will continue to produce super smart and talented individuals who will solve more mysteries of the Universe, ease our suffering and extend the longevity of our lifespan. The recent mapping of the human genome was only made possible with super computers capable of handling the sequencing of billions of DNA strands and base pairs in the human genes and cells. Now humans can alter or speed up nature's process of natural selection by cutting or adding to the gene sequence in our DNA. He might even find a way to totally eradicate cancer!

Humans are extremely adept at altering what they know, but humans will never know where DNA came from and how to create life from nothing. Tampering with the natural evolutionary process and the laws of nature through gene manipulation can have serious consequences if not done ethically. It can produce lifeforms or species that can wipe out all humankind. This may be nature's way of limiting the impact of what humans can do when we try to play God. And we can only do so much as our lifespan is too limited and short. According to the laws of nature, all living things will eventually die given enough time. Humankind is no exception. The opposite of evolution is extinction. When human beings are gone, nature will evolve back to whatever it was or will be.

My Viewpoint:

The laws of nature are immutable and hardwired in the DNA of all living things. **We can only marvel at the intelligence of creation to instill such a simple, yet so effective, set of priorities for all living entities.**

Chapter 9

WHERE DOES EVIL COME FROM?

The concepts of "good" and "evil" are human-made. _St. Augustine (354-430 AD)_ believed evil was the "absence of God." God did not purposely create evil. Evil was human's disobedience to God. It was created by humans. Evil had no independent existence, and it certainly does not exist in nature. There are no such things as good or evil acts in nature that affect plants and animals. They simply do what come naturally to them. When a tree is growing, it is competing with other trees in the forest for sunlight and nutrients in the ground. The tree that gets the nourishment from the sun would eventually block the sun from reaching the smaller plants at its base. These shaded plants could die from starvation. Is this evil? No, it's just what nature does.

When a magpie invades a robin's nest and kills and eats the young chicks, some might say that this act is cruel. But the magpie is just eating to survive. Nature can be harsh and insensitive when survival instincts are involved. Seagulls will aggressively fight amongst themselves for the scraps of fish guts being thrown overboard from the boat. They would literally try to steal the food right out of the beaks of other seagulls. We would say that this was acceptable behaviour for birds to fight and steal like this as they were just following the natural law of the survival of the fittest. Animals, like wolves, will also group together under a dominant, or "alpha", male who would usually be the strongest, or biggest or the fittest of the males. The alpha male would fight off all other wolves wanting to claim its dominant position. This power struggle to be dominant by the best of the species is nature's way to improve the species through the natural selection of the fittest. By being the alpha male, it will have access to the best females to breed with. This would ensure that superior physical genes would be passed onto future generations that will be better adapted to thrive in the everchanging living conditions. This innate need for survival is hard-wired in the DNA of all living things and the cause of the instinctive actions taken by living things to survive.

Hard-wired into all humans is not only this instinct for survival, but also the desire to be the best. Humans are instinctively competitive by nature. We are competing all the time to see who is the best, but nature ensures that only a select few can be the best. Everyone cannot be the top leaders or athletes, although everyone can aspire to be one if nature had endowed them with the genes to make them physically superior, skilled or smart enough. Mutations in the evolutionary process is nature's way to produce "super" individuals having very special talents or physical and mental attributes that others will not have. These individuals will become our best scientists, philosophers, inventors, writers and artists, musicians and athletes. All our competitive sports are "mock wars" trying to decide who will be the best with the most dominant being recognized and rewarded. This competitive instinct in humans to be the dominant leader is the main cause why conflicts and wars continue to exist in the world. It is in our nature. When wars happen, these bring into reality the real consequences of suffering and death.

Charles Darwin (1809-1882) said that this struggle for survival is usually hardest among the species that resemble each other the most, especially when they are fighting for common territories and food. We see neighbouring ant colonies of different species "go to war" against each other with the intent of totally wiping out the other. We see wolf packs, within the same species, fighting amongst themselves to gain territorial rights. We see individual animals challenging each other to be the dominant entity. Species also exist in the human race, meaning people of different races, tribes and cultures that align themselves by their beliefs, religions and countries.

How are humans different from the animals? *Sigmund Freud's (1856-1939)* studies of the unconscious mind revealed that people's actions were often the result of "animal" urges and instincts. Even though humans have the ability to reason and a conscience to determine what should be the morally right or wrong things to do, we are still animals. When threatened, our innate instincts for survival kicks in, and we will do whatever that's needed to survive, sometimes in absence of any ethics or morality.

To understand what is good and what is evil, we must first learn what is right and wrong. In our world of opposites, good and evil will always co-exist. *David Hume (1711-1776)* believed that the ability to distinguish between right or wrong was influenced by each individual's values based on his or her upbringing, cultural, education and environment. Knowing what is right or wrong are learned attributes.

Immanuel Kant (1724-1804), however, believed that the ability to tell right from wrong was just as innate as all the other attributes of reason. Everybody has "practical reason" or the intelligence that gives us the capacity to discern what is right or wrong in every case. He called this a universal "moral law" which is governed by one's conscience.

It is natural to lie, cheat and steal following the natural laws for survival. Here is an example of children "learning" what is right or wrong from their parents or peers. Under the age of four, children's minds are like blank slates. They don't know yet what should be right or wrong, good or bad. When they do something "bad", they are punished. They remember this type of consequence for being bad and they want to avoid it. It is no wonder that when asked "Who broke this vase?", most children would respond "Not me! Not me!", even if they did it. If this is not corrected early, then these norms become acceptable behaviours as they will learn that they can lie, cheat, and even kill to avoid negative consequences.

We all want to win. You see this in business where individuals may sometimes use unethical tactics to climb the corporate ladder to reach the top. You see this with people when they are in positions of power and authority, they will do whatever they can to retain their status and material wealth. There is a lot of truth in the quote from _Lord Acton (1834-1902):_ "Power corrupts. Absolute power corrupts absolutely."

Unlike the animals who can rely only on being either the strongest or the fastest, they do not have human's superior intellect and intelligence. Yet this same superiority can manifest in evil tendencies for humans to be more cunning or conniving, or manipulative to steal, lie and cheat and to commit acts of sexual misconduct for their own selfish intent and at the expense of others. As nature allows animals to kill without regrets or feelings, humans can kill selfishly for their own benefit and may even kill for just the enjoyment of it. This would be in total disregard to any morality or integrity of what is right or wrong, and without any compassion or consideration to fellow humans. These negative traits are innate instincts in all humans. The idea of the "survival of the fittest" cannot be used to condone or to justify the excesses of human greed and individual selfishness and to ignore the ethical and moral values. Humans have the capacity for love, compassion and honesty and to do what is right. That is just as innate in humans as are their instincts to be cruel and to do hurtful things in our world of opposites. To totally eradicate evil means that we must also get rid of good. That is why evil will always persist.

Despite all the evil in the world, why do humans want to do good? And what do we do with those humans who have no sense of morality or cannot understand the consequences of their bad actions? Nature has a simple solution in making such evil humans die off to make whatever suffering caused by them to be temporary. Death has its unexpected benefits. And in the classical struggle between good and evil since the beginning of recorded time, why does good always seem to overcome and defeat evil? Is this just wishful thinking? Again, the answer can be found in the laws of nature. There will always be more people wanting to do good than those who do bad and evil things. Nature dictates that only a select few become leaders by the natural selection of the fittest. The rest are destined to be followers. All of us have suffered in some form or another in our respective lives. We know why we struggled and that good deeds with compassion and support towards others will help alleviate our suffering. We feel good when we do good.

Humans are social creatures. There will always be fewer leaders and many more followers. Leaders can be good or bad. _Aristotle (384-322 BC)_ quoted: *"He who is a good ruler must first have been ruled,"* which is very wise. You cannot have compassion for people until you have experienced the suffering they had to live with. A good leader or ruler will look after his or her people and everyone will benefit. Then there are bad rulers or dictators who choose to exploit and subjugate people for their own self-interest. Fortunately, there will always be more people wanting to do good as opposed to those who would do evil to maintain their wealth and power. History has shown that when evil is too overwhelming, the oppressed people will eventually rise and overthrow the corrupt and evil leaders that are in power – in all religious, political and corporate situations. That is the survival instincts of the oppressed. Wars are also nature's way to limit human's dominance over the other living things and the environment. If this fails, then the evil ones will eventually die off. The laws of nature are so efficient.

My Viewpoint:
We all live in a world of opposites which make up our reality. We cannot know what good is unless we have experienced evil. And we can never totally get rid of evil, as this means that we must also eliminate all good. Both will continue to exist. But why does good always seem to be victorious over evil? The answer is surprisingly simple in the laws of nature and the survival of the fittest. **These laws ensure that there will always be more people who want to do good and alleviate suffering than those few bad leaders who would choose to do things for their own personal gain by oppressing and taking advantage of the people. This is a remarkable "checks and balance" mechanism nature has instilled in us.** *And if that doesn't work, then the evil ones will eventually die to start a rejuvenation process.* **This intelligence in creating such an ingenious life system could not have come from nothing.**

Chapter 10

WHAT ARE ABSOLUTE TRUTHS?

Throughout history, ancient philosophers had difficulties trying to make sense of the world they see as the Universe was constantly changing. Things that were thought to be true, like the sun revolving around the earth, proved later on to be totally false. Human knowledge added to the confusion when humans made up answers not supported by verifiable truths.

Protagoras (485-410 BC) believed that humans cannot ever know the truth about the riddles of nature and of the Universe and that there were no absolute norms for what was right or wrong.

Georg Hegel (1770-1831) established the eternal criteria for what humans can really know about the world in its constantly changing state. He believed that the basis for human cognition changed from one generation to the next, and that there were no "eternal or absolute truths" and no reason or logic unaffected by time.

Soren Kierkegaard (1813-1855) believed that rather than searching for absolute truths, it was more important to find the kind of truths that are meaningful to the life of each individual – to find _"what is the truth for me."_ Furthermore, such truths are always subjective and the really important truths are very personal. The only thing that would be existentially important was each person's own existence.

What is a truth? Despite hundreds of years of searching for truths, no acceptable answer has ever been found. Some philosophers deny there is such a thing as an absolute truth. Others say that such truths are impossible to discover, and still others would say that truth is intrinsically paradoxical and meaningless. In other words, such truths are merely reflections of what our reality may mean to each of us. Truth may be nothing more than a conceptual idea in our minds.

To be an absolute truth, it must be intrinsically independently within itself, meaning whatever it is, it will not be affected by anything else. We consider scientific truths to be absolute truths only when they are proven by mathematical theorem. It is supposedly black and white. But are they only true to us? The Universe certainly doesn't need to know any mathematical truths for it to exist.

The laws of nature that affect all living things appear to be absolute truths. Here are some other examples of possible absolute truths:

- Nothing is static in the Universe. Change is continually happening.
- Time is infinite and everlasting making all sorts of realities possible.
- Creation of the Universe has to have come from something. It did not come from nothing.
- The Universe has order and structure. It is not random chaos.
- Death is not the absolute end to Life. Our existence does not end in nothingness, as even nothingness is shown to consist of something, yet to be fully defined.

Many times, absolute truths are things that cannot be either proven nor disproven, like the existence of a God, or whether there is life existing on other planets in the Universe. Human knowledge will continue to search for new "truths". This may be an innate purpose of our lives to seek the "why" to the existential questions for our existence.

Stephen Hawking (1942-2018)
"The greatest enemy of knowledge is not ignorance, it is the illusion of knowledge."

Continued evolution and new technological discoveries in science and biology will present new truths and opportunities. This will continue as long as we exist.

My Viewpoint:
The answers to the absolute truths will never be known within our lifetime. The constantly changing Universe makes this impossible. ***New truths will continue to be discovered as advances in science and our biological evolution continue. That is the reality of our life.***

Chapter 11

TIME CONTEXT OF HUMAN EXISTENCE

To put time into context of the age of humankind, philosophical observations have only been recorded for the past 3000 years. Dinosaurs existed 70 million years ago and they became extinct 66 million years ago when a major catastrophe in the form of a giant asteroid struck earth and blotted out the sun for decades. Their fossilized bones confirmed that such large animals did exist.

Humankind first evolved from the Neanderthals 200,000 years ago and these early humanoids were replaced 35,000 years ago by the Cro-Magnon race as part of the homo sapiens species. We are their direct descendants. The age and evolution of humankind has really been very short in terms of cosmic time. The knowledge gained from scientific and technological advances, has exploded exponentially from just the past 200 years. Yet the more we know, the more we don't know.

According to the historical timelines stated in the Bible, it is believed that God created the earth 6000 years ago. Charles Darwin believed it to be much longer at 300 million years. Today, science has estimated the earth to be about 4.5 billion years old! The age of the Universe is estimated to be 13.8 billion years old! To put this into perspective, this dwarfs the total age of humankind and the average lifespan of human beings to be less than 100 years. How does 100 years compare with the 4.5 billion years it took for earth to evolve, or the 13.8 billion years since the genesis of the Big Bang and the Universe? Our existence is insignificant, a mere blip in time. It is nothing. We still don't know if there are other Universes far older than ours that we can see with our technology. From the Universe's perspective, humankind's time and existence cannot be compared with the infinity of cosmic time.

My Viewpoint:

The modern-day humans have only been evolving on earth during the past 35,000 years. This time is absolutely insignificant when compared with the 4.5 billion years it took for the earth to become what it is today. **Where the evolution of humankind will go and how long our existence will be sustained remain unknown.**

Chapter 12

WHAT IS EVERLASTING?

D o you really want to live forever? To have everlasting life and to avoid death go totally against the laws of nature. Who really wants to live forever? 200 years ago, the average life span was only about 30 years. Now with the medical advances made in the biological sciences, one can expect to live to 100 years and more. How long, then, is long? 200 years? 500 years? To make eternal life work, everyone needs to age longer together. Otherwise, the one with eternal life will be isolated and alone while everyone else dies off. Those in ancient times who had searched for the fountain of youth were the ones with power and wealth who wanted to prolong their enjoyment by living as long as possible. They did not think through what negative consequences there may be to live forever. Ageing and the associated decay will slowly continue. Death can be delayed, but never stopped. Once we have done it all, and have attained more wealth and power than we need to survive and learned everything that's needed to know, then what? We can get used to too much of the same thing, including longevity. And we cannot take our wealth and status with us when we die. Humans need challenges and conflicts to make us feel "alive" and to make our lives purposeful.

Immanuel Kant (1724-1804) said we cannot expect to understand what we are. Maybe we can comprehend a flower or an insect, but never ourselves, and less even can we expect to comprehend the Universe. He believed that there was no certain knowledge to be obtained on the "big" philosophical questions whether humans can have an immortal soul, or whether there is a God, or whether nature consists of tiny indivisible particles, and whether the Universe is finite or infinite. To answer these, reason must operate beyond the limits of what we humans can comprehend. However, we continue to seek answers about a totality of which we ourselves are just a miniscule part of. We can never know this totality because of our limited sensory perception and reason. This makes our search for such answers to be futile.

WHAT IS EVERLASTING?

The Universe is ever-changing. Nothing is static. Infinity is a mind-boggling concept to grasp as we have never experienced it, nor will we ever see it. Here is an example showing how difficult it is to understand the magnitude of how limitless infinity can be. Think of the Universe as a vast ocean that holds all the secrets of creation and life. In the last 100 years, the scientific and technological advances have increased our human knowledge exponentially well beyond what have been accumulated in the last 3000 years. Think of the totality of this knowledge as being represented by a single drop of water. In the next 100 years, we may become more knowledgeable enough to make two more drops of water. At this rate, will we ever learn the truth? How can three drops of water define the totality of the ocean and its creation? Infinity has no meaning or reality that can be understood by us.

This is the reason why most people don't want to talk or even think about Life and Death as it puts too much effort searching for answers to the unknown. When we meet, we don't say, "Hi. What do you think is going to happen to you when you die?" The meaning of life is very personal. Someone once said: "It hurts my brain trying to find answers to questions which cannot be answered. It is a waste of my time!" We'd rather talk about things in our daily lives that we think we can control. We complain about things that negatively impacts our lives. It is a bit ironic that we spend so little time contemplating our mortality and how we should try to live our lives. Maybe this is nature's way to ease our angst of the unknown by making our daily struggles consume the majority of our efforts and thoughts.

Death is the great common denominator and equalizer. It doesn't matter whether you are rich or poor, powerful or ordinary. You cannot take your material wealth and status of power and prestige with you when you die. You will die the same way you were born, with nothing. You can be remembered by the legacy you leave behind to those who loved you or benefited from your short existence. However, that too, in time, will disappear.

My Viewpoint:
Nobody lives forever, and why would anyone want to? Death is the common denominator for everyone. You cannot take your wealth and status with you when you die. If you want to enjoy life a little longer, then take care of your physical and mental health. **Do the things in life that are meaningful to you and that will bring happiness to you and to those around you.**

Chapter 13

WHY ARE MEN AND WOMEN SO DIFFERENT?

---

*H*eraticlus (540-480 BC)* first pointed out that our world is characterized by opposites. You wouldn't know peace without war, or good from bad. Without this constant interplay of opposites, the world would cease to exist. In religions, this is known as Dualism: the theological doctrine that there are two eternal principles – one good and one evil. *St. Augustine (354-430)* recognized the dualisms that exist in the world – good and evil, lightness and darkness, spirit and matter. This was reinforced by *Georg Hegel (1770-1831)* who believed that our reality is only valid when it is characterized by opposites.

In science and nature, opposites exist naturally. _Sir Isaac Newton's (1643-1727)_ Third Law of Motion states: _"For every action (force) in nature, there is an equal and opposite reaction."_ Magnetism has equal and opposite poles and magnets can attract and repel themselves depending on their polarity – like men and women. The natural attraction is so strong when coupled together they become very difficult to pull apart. By nature's design, men and women complement each other. The two are needed for pro-creation. Men and women can be considered to be opposites in their traits, but as human beings we are the same. The male gender is just a variant version of the basic female form. Is this another profound truth? While men and women have noted differences, we share much in common that make us the same.

At this point, I must interject with a story about men and women and who is the smarter sex. At a company function that included husbands and wives, the president was making a speech to the assembly, basically telling everyone how great and smart he was for building the company to the success it had achieved. He was obviously the alpha male. There was some truth in what he was saying, but he wasn't entirely accurate. So, I got up and said a few words after his speech. I said that he wasn't giving his wife much credit for his success and that in truth, she was actually smarter than he was. I said that I had asked my son, who is a doctor, "Where does intelligence come from?", and he answered, "It comes from the X chromosome." From my logical reasoning as an engineer, I reminded everyone that a man is made up of X-Y chromosomes, while a woman is X-X chromosomes. This means that women have twice the smart genes than men. I didn't say that all women are smarter than men, only that women inherently have twice the capacity to be smarter! The women in the audience loved my logic. Furthermore, to prove that women are indeed smarter, I asked, "Who typically dies first? The man or the woman? And when the husband dies, who inherits everything the man has worked so hard to achieve?" Women are smart to be rewarded by letting their husbands stress themselves out working so hard. By this time, all the ladies were clapping and cheering, including his wife. My boss didn't know how to respond. He was flabbergasted. In hindsight, I guess maybe this was why I never became a vice-president in the company. Oh well. That's life. It was meant to be.

Georg Hegel (1770-1831) said _"the difference between man and woman is like that between animals and plants. Men correspond to animals, while women correspond to plants because their development is more placid and influenced by feelings, whereas manhood is attained by stress of thought and much technical exertion."_

WHY ARE MEN AND WOMEN SO DIFFERENT?

Men and women have obvious physical differences, but where we really differ is in our values and the way we think. Throughout history, men have never fully understood women. When asked what he thinks of most, _Stephen Hawking (1942-2018)_ said: _"Women ... they are a complete mystery!"_ It can be argued whether men are superior to women, or vice-versa, as our innate characteristics are so different. But opposites must exist as that is our reality.

To illustrate the difference, a man and a woman will react quite differently when offered a position of power and authority. It has been my observation that a man would jump at the chance of such a promotion even if he knew he was woefully unqualified for the position. A woman, however, would be more thoughtful whether she could do the job or really wanted it, and how she and others might feel about it. She would have no problem or regrets declining the position. History has shown that a woman ruler or leader will be much different than a man. A woman does not aspire to reach for the top and to be the "alpha" dominant position. Of course, there will always be exceptions when we see the occasional women with the ambitions of men.

Here is a feminine perspective from the philosopher:

WHY ARE MEN AND WOMEN SO DIFFERENT?

Simone de Beauvoir (1908-1986)
"In our culture, women are treated as the second sex. Men behave as if they are the subjects, treating women like their objects, thus depriving them of the responsibility for their own life."

The following lists some of the traditional distinct and opposite characteristics of women and men. Many of these traits may seem outdated and even politically incorrect. From a historical context, they showed that the perceived differences can be very pronounced. Of course, there will always be exceptions to this listing.

Woman	Man
Nurturing and caring	Provider and protector
Democratic	Autocratic
Passive	Aggressive
Attuned to feelings	Results/action oriented
Compassionate	Insensitive
Thoughtful	Logic driven
The "gentle" sex	Physical strength
Team oriented	Individual (self)
Receptive	Forceful

One last observation about men and women. You may have seen the movie Jerry McGuire where he said to his wife, *"You complete me."* Successful couples who stay together for a long time are never 100% compatible. Opposites do attract, but to be lasting, it is my opinion, based on my relationship with my wife, that it is more like 50-60% compatible - enough to see things alike and be attracted to each other, but different enough to make life interesting. And contrary to what men think that they are the skillful ones in wooing and catching a woman, it is the woman who decides who her future mate will be. As in nature, it is the female species that decides which males will mate with her! The woman will typically choose a mate that will have some qualities she doesn't have, but her partner will have, so as "to complete" them both. Simple enough.

My Viewpoint:
Women will always be an enigma to men. _Blame nature for this. Men will never truly understand how women really think. It is amazing how the laws of nature would purposely make men and women so different, yet so attractive to each other. This world of opposites is our reality and these differences make our life interesting and worth living. If men and women cannot solve the mysteries of each other, then what hopes have we to solve the riddles of Life and the Universe?_

Chapter 14

SCIENCE AS THE "NEW RELIGION"

This brings the philosophical history to current times where continuing advances in science will expand our knowledge and new truths will be discovered. These will change the way we view the existential philosophical questions: "Who are we?" and "What is this world we live in?"

The search for these answers will always be an integral part and purpose of our life. New scientific knowledge and our ongoing evolution will open new frontiers of opportunities in this constantly changing Universe. However, spirituality must not be forgotten, nor ignored by new insights and discoveries of science.

Albert Einstein (1879-1955)

"The religion of the future will be a cosmic religion. It should transcend a personal god and avoid dogmas and theology. Covering both natural and spiritual, it should be based on a religious sense arising from the experience of all things, natural and spiritual and a meaningful unity."

The "mathematical method" of reasoning will dominate over unproven beliefs based on faith and religion. Philosophical truths will be proven in the same way one proves a mathematical theorem. Only reasoning substantiated by proven scientific truths can give us certainty. Science through Einstein's theory of relativity showed the interdependence of gravity, space and time and that our Universe is neither eternal nor static. According to the general theory of relativity, there must have been a state of infinite density at the beginning of time before the Big Bang causing our expanding universe. As in our world of opposites, given enough time, there must also be a state of an equivalent Big Crunch where the whole universe will re-collapse back to its initial singularity. This means our Universe may continuously evolve in this recurring cycle, first expanding and then contracting. Throughout these cycles, there will be birth and death cycles of stars and planetary systems in the Universe. Are there also multiple Universes beyond our own that we cannot see? Are there other humans like us somewhere out in the

Universe? With infinite time, the logical answer to such possibilities is that anything is possible.

Stephen Hawking (1942-2018): Quantum theory of gravity – one that combines the general theory of relativity (gravity and the macro universe) with quantum mechanics (atoms and the micro universe) to result in a comprehensive unified theory of the universe. When this happens, this Unifying Theory of Everything will open up new truths and possibilities and create a new era of knowledge and understanding. Combining quantum mechanics with general relativity creates the possibility that time and space together might form a new fourth dimension which will be much different to our current realities. This 4th dimension already exists in our minds. We can already travel to far off galaxies in our minds and imagine things that are not possible today. Our realities can be endless.

Science has determined that the nothingness seen by the ancient philosophers is actually something. This black nothingness or emptiness in space are actually dark matter and dark energy which cannot be seen, but they nevertheless exist. We now see black holes and how the power of infinite gravity can warp time and make light disappear. Nothing cannot come from nothing. Even nothing comes from something! However, science does not have the answers to everything. Scientific legitimacy is limited to the observable physical world. The subject of feelings, thoughts, values and aspirations are not governed by science. Reality is so much more complex than the objective scientific observations of material things.

Quantum mechanics is the study of all things at the atomic and sub-atomic level, or our micro-universe. It is the key to our understanding of the workings of creation which the ancient philosophers already knew when they said all things came "from atoms". This is where creation originates. To know the secrets of creation is as the philosophers would say "to know the mind of God." Here is a description of quantum mechanics which puts it into the reality we are accustomed to. When Michelangelo carved out his famous statue of David from a slab of marble, he saw in his mind the figure in the block and proceeded to chip away the marble that weren't part of the statue. All his senses were used. He would think of what he needed to do, calculate the dimensions, see the form being revealed, touch the smoothness of the marble, hear the hammer and chisels chipping away, and taste and smell the fine marble dust in the air. He made the statue using his senses and knowledge of how it was to be done. This is the reality we know. Now consider that instead of a block of marble, you were given a pile of microscopic marble dust and were asked to make the same statue from these tiny particles. This is the quantum mechanics way to make something real from atoms and molecules.

We simply do not have the knowledge nor technology to build such a statue this way, let alone trying to create something alive from scratch.

To understand the genesis of the Universe at the Big Bang, Einstein's general theory of relativity must align with quantum mechanics. They do not at present. The theory of relativity suggests that the accurate calculation of the precise condition of the cosmos at any time can be calculated if sufficient data exists. But quantum mechanics asserts that the world of microscopic particles can only be understood in probabilistic terms and the data is never precisely accurate as the fundamental building blocks or quanta of matter are subject to the "uncertainty principle" that cannot be precisely calculated mathematically. The uncertainty principle states that reality at the fundamental level of the atomic structure, where creation occurs, is indeterminate, unpredictable and probabilistic. Quantum mechanics tell us that it is impossible to accurately predict how a particle might behave in a given situation. One can know at any one time where an electron is, but not what it is doing, or knowing what it is doing, but not where it is. That is the uncertainty principle and the conundrum that science and mathematics have not been able to solve how a single atom works, let alone the entire Universe.

There is a vast unknown as to the potential of the human brain and where its evolution will take it. Through MRI imaging, we know that the whole brain is active, but only a maximum of 16% is ever used at any time. This is because the billions of neurons in our brains require a lot of our body energy to function and it is currently limited to consuming only 20% of it. Imagine what might be possible if the majority of our body energy can be directed to the brain. Maybe in the future, humans will evolve to be able to read minds or to communicate by thoughts, and to physically move objects by tele-kinesis in projecting physical force via the mind like Darth Vader in Star Wars, or being able to really extend our chi in Tai Chi! Advances in the science of neurobiological structures and the bio-chemical functions have helped map the brain to search where our consciousness reside. The nature of consciousness is the key characteristic that makes humans sentient. The qualities of the mind have the potential for limitless development and ways may be found to transform or reduce the effects of negative emotional traits and to eliminate inherent genetic disabilities. Of course, all genetic modifications must be done morally and ethically. Humans cannot play God.

Meditation can lead to enlightenment, but it is difficult to learn and to do properly. The left part of the brain is associated with positive emotions like happiness, joy and contentment. This implies that happiness can be cultivated through mental training of the brain to reach that inner peace of mind. Our normal everyday state of mind tends to be tied either to recollections of the past or to hopes and fears about the future. We tend to live either in the past or in the future and very rarely in the present. Proper meditation through practice and determination will allow one to reach the required state of mind devoid of any specific or determinable content. This stage of "mindfulness" provides a highly refined sensitivity to everything that happens, however minute, in one's surroundings and in one's mind. Mindfulness allows the prolonged attention and the resulting clarity from the single pointed concentration that is necessary to attain enlightenment.

Dalai Lama (1935-Present)
On Enlightenment*: "Bringing order out of chaos, light out of darkness, day out of night and existence out of nothingness."*

We should not be overly concerned about the current fears of global warming and climate change being catastrophes that will devastate and destroy all life. These issues will only be addressed when all humankind is directly threatened by specific events. Then, humans will do whatever that is necessary to ensure its survival. Humans have proven to be very resilient and adaptable. Humans are very adept in taking proven mathematical and scientific truths and converting them to technological advances to alter our living conditions and surroundings. If Nature wanted to destroy earth and all living things, it could do so a thousand times better than any human being can do. There are many natural disasters which humans cannot stop, such as earthquakes and volcanic eruptions, weather extremes like drought, floods, fire, hurricanes and tornadoes, and the rise and fall of ocean levels due to the cyclic ice ages since the evolution of the earth. When disasters strike, humans will simply continue to adapt to survive.

Nor should we be overly concerned about the advances made in artificial intelligence (AI) and the fear that machines will become so smart and powerful that they will overtake and dominate human beings. The domination part might happen as machines can learn from us how to dominate others. But this rudimentary human knowledge transferred to machines will never be adequate to do anything that will affect or control the Universe. Machines cannot be better than humans when their existence initially started from the totality of human knowledge. Just as humans cannot be a God, neither can machines. Machines will never acquire the innate instincts for "survival at all cost" hard-wired into human beings and all living things. You have to feel suffering and machines have no feelings. If humans fail to survive, so will the machines that humans created. Our innate instinct for survival will never let machines dominate or destroy humankind.

Humans are very adept in solving physical and biological problems mathematically and then manipulating the results to change the environment. The internet and wireless communications have been solved mathematically. One of the reasons why nuclear cold fusion does not exist to give humanity an environmentally safe and unlimited source of energy equivalent to the intensity of the sun, is that it has not been solved mathematically despite efforts to do so in the past 50 years. The solution will come one day and we already have developed the technology needed to harness and control nuclear energy. Similarly, quantum mechanics will one day make teleportation a reality when we learn the secrets of our existence at the atomic and subatomic levels.

Here is a list of the expected scientific advances which are possible given our unique evolution and ability to change and control our environment. In time, continuing technological discoveries will allow some of these future possibilities to become commonplace realities. Some are already in progress. Who can say what will happen in the next 3000 years? 50 years ago, we didn't know that the discovery of electricity would lead to the internet and the wireless communications so prevalent now. One day, we will end our current concerns about climate change and the destruction of our environment when we solve the mysteries of nuclear cold fusion and have access to limitless and clean energy. That will be the next big technological breakthrough that will trigger a paradigm shift which will fundamentally change the science of all things. Human civilizations will continue to survive and thrive. There is so much potential for humankind.

- Artificial intelligence
- Robots and automation
- Synthetic biology
- Genome manipulation and cloning
- Genetic engineering
- Neuro biology and neuroscience
- Maximizing the potentials of the brain
- Telekinesis (mind control)
- Wireless and telepathic communications
- Teleportation
- The Unifying Theory of Everything
- Unlocking the secrets of Quantum Mechanics
- Nanotechnology (building with atoms and molecules)
- Nuclear fusion (harnessing the energy of the sun)
- Travel at light speed
- Space travel and colonization of planets
- Time travel
- Longevity through bionics (the modern fountain of youth)
- Mastering gravitation

- Understanding dark matter and dark energy
- Cure for cancer and other diseases (slowing the aging process)
- Control of the weather (global warming, floods, cold, heat, wind)
- Food production and population control

Spirituality through religious and philosophical insights will continue to be essential to support our mental health as everyone needs to believe in something that will give us a reason for living. However, faith alone does not create anything tangible that will affect our physical reality and environment. Science, as the new religion, will produce results that we can see and experience, that are real and are backed by proven mathematical truths. These technological and biological changes have the potential to make our world a totally different and better place to live. We should marvel at what humankind has done in such a short time, and where our evolution might take us.

However, science cannot proceed without spirituality. Technological and scientific advances must be done in a moral and ethical manner, doing the right things and not building weapons of mass destruction and for killing. Ethics is also needed in genetic cloning and manipulation. The relationship between our knowledge and power must align with the responsibility to do what is right and ethical. Science and spirituality share the same goal, which is the betterment of humanity.

Dalai Lama (1935-Present)
"The higher the level of knowledge and power, the greater the sense of moral responsibility needed. This should be the basis for human ethics."

The next 3000 years will no doubt bring many of these possibilities to reality. However, creation and the workings of the Universe will remain unsolved as we will never find the answers in our lifetime. The more we learn and know through science, the more we don't know. Yet we persist in searching for answers. That is the enigma of our Life.

My Viewpoint:
The technical advances in the physical and biological sciences continue to be breathtaking in their scope and potential to improve our living conditions and long-term health. The mysteries of Life continue to be unlocked. But ***science cannot advance without spirituality in doing the right things, morally and ethically.*** *Otherwise, consequences can be dire when science is mis-used.* ***We are entering a wonderful era when science and technology expands our knowledge to realize the amazing possibilities for our future.***

Chapter 15

CONCLUSION

By this time, you should have come to the conclusion the philosophers already knew, that there are really no definitive answers to all the eternal philosophical questions. Existential questions cannot be answered once and for all. The Universe is constantly evolving, as well as our knowledge and truths. I used to be a pantheist, believing in God as the Supreme Being and creator of everything. But as I aged and became presumably wiser, I have become an agnostic who is also a scientist and fatalist. Someone once told me that science is my religion. Quite a combination. What are you now?

I have realized that the more I know, the more I don't know and will never know in my lifetime. We simply won't live long enough. No doubt, you have personally seen or experienced many of the things discussed in this book. Hopefully, you have gained some better insights and understanding of why things are the way they are, and will continue to be so.

As _Socrates (470-399 BC)_ so wisely said:
"One thing only I know, and that is that I know nothing."

A philosophical question is by definition something that each generation, each individual, must ask over and over again. A true philosopher is one who comes with utterly no pre-conceived opinions. He or she is like the child who perceives the world as it is, without putting more into things being experienced. We must also be childlike to see the marvels of creation and the wonders of the Universe.

Despite inequalities of wealth, class, health, physical, racial and cultural characteristics, all humans are born with the same basic equality of our human nature and desires. We all possess certain potentialities, cognitive and physical abilities and dispositions, and the right to seek happiness and to alleviate suffering. All human beings have an equal value and the innate potential for goodness.

Jean-Paul Sartre (1905-1980) said it is useless to search for the meaning of life when we don't know what we don't know or where we are going. We are constantly improvising and searching to determine how we are to live our lives. We will never truly know the purpose of our existence. Our lives mean nothing to the Universe. It only means something to us. Our existence came from seemingly nothingness and at death, we will go back to where it all started.

Ludwig Wittgenstein (1889-1951) challenged the need and methodology of Western philosophy. He rejected traditional philosophy as it wasn't giving us the kind of knowledge expected. He argued that there cannot be any philosophical "truths" that is derived from facts that are not open to the methods of science and that any results based on intuition, or pure reasoning, or conceptual analysis would only lead to confused and wishful thinking. Philosophy is supposed to provide some fundamental insights into the human character and conditions and contribute to our understanding the nature of the Universe and the meaning of our existence. Philosophers cannot explain the workings of science, nor should they attempt to do so as wrong conclusions may be drawn. Where science cannot answer, then insights from philosophers, and similarly from religions, can play important roles to ease our fears of the unknown and to help us make some sense of it all.

When people realize that they will one day die, and having no meaning to cling to, they experience existential angst, that nothing is real and that life has neither meaning nor purpose. Like the world of opposites, you have two fundamental choices – whether to look at your life positively and strive to make the best of your existence, or to be pessimistic of your life and be fearful of what will happen to you after death. You are guaranteed to die, and worrying just adds to your angst and mental suffering. Death should not be a concern to such an extent. Here is a sage quote:

Epicurus (341-270 BC) : *"Death does not concern us, because as long as we exist, death is not here. And when it comes, we no longer exist. The gods are not to be feared. Death is nothing to worry about. Good is easy to attain. The fearful is easy to endure. To live a good life, it is important to overcome the fear of death."*

Acceptance of life for what it is, and not what it should be, can be attained when one simply accepts Life for all it is. *Deepak Chopra's (1947-present)* Law of Acceptance puts this acceptance in the right context. To paraphrase:

You are exactly where you are supposed to be. All your past decisions and events, whether good or bad, have led you to precisely this point in time. Accept that it is what it is and that you cannot change the past. Remember the famous quote from _Shakespeare (1564-1616):_ _"What's done cannot be undone."_ And don't blame others including yourself for your situation, even if there is justification. **The Universe has unfolded exactly in the way it should.** So, who are you to argue with the Universe? Having such acceptance opens the possibility of what actions you can take going forward in your life and how you can be responsible to make things better for yourself and for those around you. This will lead to your own path to happiness.

Buddha (563-483 BC)
"If one wishes to avoid certain types of results, one needs to change the conditions that give rise to them. This includes changing the condition of one's own state of mind."

Jean-Paul Sartre (1905-1980)
"Life must have a meaning. It is an imperative. But we ourselves must create this meaning in our own lives. To exist is to create your own life."

To live a good life, accept that:

- You are unique in having your own special relationship with the Universe.
- Your life is insignificant and what you do and what you leave behind have absolutely no lasting impact to the workings and existence of the Universe.
- Your life, for however long or short it may be, is definitely significant to you and to all the other living things around you.
- Everyone seeks personal happiness and less suffering in life. How you attain this goal is within your control, based on your morality and free will.
- Helping others to attain their happiness will result in a better world with less suffering.
- You will truly never know the workings of the Universe and creation, so don't worry about it or fear the unknown prospects of Death.
- You live in a world of unknowns. Open your eyes to the good things in Life. Marvel at the wonders and beauty of the Universe.

Unfortunately, evil will continue to exist as long as the laws of nature for survival instinctively guide the actions of humankind. The good part is that these same laws will ensure that there will always be more people wanting to do good and live a harmonious life free of suffering than those who hold the opposite view. Good will continue to triumph over evil.

Here is a final thought on Life and Death. Life can be a struggle, but look at it positively as our future is promising and full of amazing possibilities. Humans will continue to evolve and to strive to live a better life. That is the nature of human beings and the purpose of our life. There is so much yet to see and to discover. This gift of Life to us is remarkable.

J.R. Tolkein (1892-1973)
On Death: *"The gift of the One to Man, it is bitter to receive. Death is truly God's gift. Death is the one unknown, a new, unexpected discovery. The loss and the silence of Death – it is our curse, but also our blessing."*

I hope that some of the insights on Life have resonated with you to explain why life, your life, is the way it is. Live life to the fullest. Everyone has their own unique talents. Everyone is good at something. Your life is special to you. Don't take Life for granted. Make it meaningful to you as only you will know what life and happiness will be for you. And if you are fortunate to grow old, consider it to be a gift and a privilege that not everyone gets. Embrace this time you are alive. Your life is precious as it may be the only time you are you!

<u>My Final Viewpoint:</u>
It is a great time to be alive. Strive to live a good life. Take time to appreciate the wonders of creation and the Universe. Don't take Life for granted. There is so much more of Life to experience. Your life can be so positive. ***Death is not an ending, but a possible new beginning of untold wonders yet to be discovered. Look forward to the exciting journey beyond Life when your time comes.***

EPILOGUE

I started the book with an ancient quote that depicted the harsh reality of Life. I tried hard to maintain a positive outlook on Life, especially when we are so insignificant in our Universe, and our existence seemed meaningless. Then an epiphany came to me to realize that Life is truly a gift. We shouldn't take it for granted by dwelling on the negative aspects of life and the "sufferings" we have had to endure. In our world of opposites, more often than not, we fail to see the positives in Life, to take the time to see the stars at night, in silence, to think about the complexities of living things, to smell the fragrance of the apple blossoms, to see the smiles and hear the laughter from the people we love, to "feel" our presence as an integral and active part of nature and the world we live in.

Technology has recently allowed us to take high resolution pictures of the surface of the sun, something we have never been able to see before. It is amazing to see how the surface patterns are so randomly uniform, yet definitely structured as if the surface of the sun was purposely designed to be like this. There are other similar structures on earth that mirror this uniform randomness, like the striking columnar patterns seen at the Giant's Causeway in Ireland, or the unique crystalline patterns of snowflakes. It just confirms that there is an intelligence in creation that we can not even imagine. Such marvels of creation are all around us!

I leave you with a positive thought. This is my favorite quote to reflect the wonders of Life:

Richard Feynman (1918-1988)
"I wonder why, I wonder why I wonder why I wonder?
I wonder WHY I wonder why,
I WONDER WHY I WONDER!!"

I am wiser now, and more enlightened. I hope you are, too!

POSTSCRIPT

In this section, the philosophical content come from the book, "Sophie's World – A Novel About the History of Philosophy", which is an international best seller, translated in 64 languages. This book was written in 1991 by *Jostein Gaarder (1952-Present)*, a philosophy teacher and writer from Oslo, Norway. It details the philosophical thoughts of the great philosophers of Western civilization over the past 3000 years.

There are many quotes included from the great philosophers of Asia who influenced the Eastern civilization - like Rumi, Lao Tzu (Taoism) and Confucius. Buddhism and Hinduism are mentioned as their beliefs and philosophy on how to live a good and moral life align with the theological ideals of the Western religions of Christianity, Judaism and Islam.

The thoughts on science and spirituality and the tenets of Buddhism come from the book, "The Universe in a Single Atom – The Convergence of Science and Spirituality" by the 14th Dalai Lama (Tenzin Gyatso).

CHRONOLOGY OF PHILOSOPHERS

<u>Ancient Times</u> (BC to 1100 AD)
Buddha (563-483 BC)
Lao Tzu (5th Century BC)
Thales of Miletus (625-545 BC)
Anaximander of Miletus (610-547 BC)
Anaximenes of Miletus (570-526 BC)
Confucius (551-479 BC)
Parmenides (540-480 BC)
Heraclitus of Ephesus (540-480 BC)
Empedocles (490-430 BC)
Anaxagoras (500-428 BC)
Protagoras of Abdera (485-410 BC)
Democritus of Abdera (460-370 BC)
Socrates (470-399 BC)
Antisthenes (455-360 BC)
Plato (428-347 BC)
Aristotle (384-322 BC)
Epicurus (341-270 BC)
Plotinus (270-205 BC)
Jesus Christ (5 BC–33 AD)
St. Paul (5-65 AD)
St. Augustine (354-430 AD)

Middle or Dark Ages (1100-1453)
Rumi (1207-1273)
St. Thomas Aquinas (1225-1274)

The Renaissance Period (1400-1600)
Reformation Period (1517-1648)
Martin Luther (1483-1546)
Thomas Hobbes (1588-1679)

Baroque Period (1600-1750)
Rene Descartes (1596-1650)
Baruch Spinoza (1632-1677)
John Locke (1632-1704)
David Hume (1711-1776)
George Berkeley (1685-1753)

French Enlightenment Period (1700-1800)
Industrial Revolution (1760-1830)
Immanuel Kant (1724-1804)

Romanticism Period (1800-1850)
Friedrich Schelling (1775-1854)
Georg Wilhelm Friedrich Hegel (1770-1831)
Soren Kierkegaard (1813-1855)
Karl Marx (1818-1883)
Charles Darwin (1809-1882)
Sigmund Freud (1856-1939)
Friedrich Nietzsche (1844-1900)

<u>Age of Science</u> (From 1900)
Albert Einstein (1879-1955)
Ludwig Wittgenstein (1889-1951)
Jean-Paul Sartre (1905-1980)
Simone de Beauvoir (1908-1986)
Stephen Hawking (1942-2018)
14th Dalai Lama (1935-Present)

SECTION II

MY CONCLUSIONS ON FATE, DEATH AND THE MEANING OF LIFE

PREAMBLE

I had initially written this essay six years ago. It was only five pages long and my conclusions on life were very negative. I had concluded then, that life was so insignificant it didn't matter whether I was a serial killer or virtuous like Mother Teresa. At the end, I was going to be dead. I guess I was a nihilist then, who believed that "nothing matters". So why bother trying to live a good and moral life when there didn't seem to be any meaningful purpose in life! I might as well just slit my wrists and end it all.

Then a thought flashed before me and I remembered the haunting lyrics from the famous song:

Is That All There Is? - Peggy Lee (1920-2002)

"If that's the way you feel about it, why don't you just end it all.
Oh no, not me. I'm in no hurry for that final disappointment.
And when it comes and I am breathing my last breath, I'll be saying to myself ....
Is that all there is, is that all there is.
If that's all there is, my friends, then let's keep dancing, let's break out the booze and have a ball.
If that's all there is."

I have always been an optimistic and positive person, looking for the good in people and the beauty all around us. I could not leave the impression that there was nothing worthwhile to look forward to in life. On the contrary, there is so much to live for.

As a result, I re-wrote this essay to reflect who I really am and what the meaning of Life can be. I hope my views and outlook on Life are similar to yours.

FATE AND DEATH

D o you believe in Fate? How things happen in our lives because they were meant to be? I believe there is a randomness in Life that we simply cannot control. You walk along a crowded street milling with people and a heavy object falls out of the sky. And of all the people around you, it strikes you, just you, and it kills you instantly. Now you are dead. You take the same subway to work every day at the same time in London at the King's Crossing Station, and on that day, terrorists had planted a bomb in the very train you normally take. But you missed it as your travelling companion was just a little bit late joining you that morning because his alarm clock did not go off, or something trivial like that. So, you live. This is a real case, as that person who so luckily survived is my eldest son. A mother and her six years old daughter are enjoying a leisurely lunch at the outdoor patio of a restaurant. They are happy and laughing. A marble slab on the building wall 12 stories up becomes loose and falls down, killing the little girl in front of her horrified mother. Or you are this tiny ant scurrying across the sidewalk, bothering no one and minding your own business, and someone steps on you and squishes the life out of you. All of these incidents have occurred in real life. Why is it like this?

Some call such incidents good luck when fortunate things happen. Others call it bad luck when tragedy strikes and there is no rational reason why this had to happen to you. This is Fate. Some say that your lifespan and when you are going to die have already been written in the future and that the events which occurred in the past, and those yet to be realized in the future, have already been mapped out. Sure, you can say that you are in control of your destiny and that you can do things to ensure that you will live longer – like exercising regularly and eating healthier, and not doing drugs or pursuing a life of crime. But Fate has already factored these in as it knows when your time is up. My Father, _Albert Yep (1922-1999)_ said it best, _"When it is time for you to go, it is time for you to go."_ That young girl was meant to die. It was her time. And there was nothing anyone could have done to prevent it. We might ask then, "Why did she have to die? What did she do to deserve to die? Did she enjoy her life? And at such a tender age, what was the purpose of her life?" At the end, she is dead and there seem to be no meaning to her existence.

So, isn't this a very pessimistic way of looking at Life? That it doesn't matter what you do in life because at the end, we will all be dead? Well, in truth ... yes, because in time, we will all die. It is inevitable. That is Life, and Death is our ultimate fate, our destiny. We just don't know when we are going to die. So, we continue living our lives without ever truly thinking of death, especially when we are young, brimming with energy and high expectations of what our lives might bring or become. We have goals to pursue and important things to be done. We are too busy living our lives, so consumed with our day-to-day issues that we don't have time to even think about where our Life is leading us. But as we get older and have encountered tragedies close to home, or see Death lurking in the shadows of our mortality, we begin to wonder how much longer do we really have left? Is there more to this life of ours after death? We question whether we have lived a good life. Have we done things in our lives which have made any difference to anyone or anything? And when we are dead, does it really matter what we did during our lives? We question "what is the purpose of this life we are living?" and "what happens after we die?". Serious questions which are not easily answered, so we don't think about it.

If we knew exactly when in the future we were going to die, would it change the way we would live? I would argue yes. If you had terminal cancer and were given only two years left to live, would you not try to cram a whole lifetime in your remaining years while you can? There is bliss in this ignorance of not knowing when your time will come. It lets you continue living your life as you currently do now without any fear or thought about

Death ... until one gets really old or really sick, or when someone close to you dies.

THE ROAD OF LIFE

To understand Death, we must look at Life and what life means to us. One way of looking at Life is pictorially as multiple pathways, or events, between two major points in your life. The starting point will be Life, and the ending point will be Death. That is all we know for sure. These will be the only fixed points and the events in between are our collective experiences which we try to understand our world within the limited confines of our consciousness. If we consider Life and Death to be absolutes, then anything "alive" must eventually die. So what does "being alive" mean to you? Some might say that being alive means that you have a soul and that you will continue to live, or exist, in some other form after we die. Many religions subscribe to this belief – that life is eternal. But do animals and plants which are also alive have souls too? Here is a definition on being "alive" based on scientific observations and studies. It ties in with the question, "Why do we need sleep?"

Despite all the years in the scientific study of sleep, we still haven't figured out why all living things must sleep.

Some say that sleep allows our bodies to rebalance and detox our systems. This may be nature's way to "recharge" ourselves to continue living. An expert sleep psychologist was once asked, "What is an absolute fact that you know to be true about sleep?" His answer was, "If you don't get enough sleep, you will surely die." Is that all? He still couldn't give any scientific explanation why we and every other living thing must sleep. They had run experiments on mice where they deprived them of sleep. The mice had to stay awake by walking on a treadmill and if they stopped to go to sleep, they were dunked into water to wake them up. This cycle repeated itself for days until the poor mice died. The autopsy showed that the mice were perfectly healthy and fully functional. They simply died from exhaustion from the lack of sleep. So a scientific definition of what is "alive" can be stated as anything that needs to sleep or has a sleep, or dormant, cycle. This would include us, all animals, fish, insects, plants and micro-organisms. A rock would not be considered to be alive, but in the following discussion on the universe, matter and infinite time, the rock may evolve into something living, given enough time to do so.

Going back to Life and Death, between these two points, you will have many connecting lines. Call them the pathways we choose to take, based on the decisions we make during our lives. And within these pathways, there will be many other interconnecting lines. You probably know these as "the forks in the paths on your Road of Life." We make choices in our lives each time we reach a "fork" and we have to decide which path to take. Whichever one we choose, we must endure whatever consequences, good or bad, arising from that decision we made until we reach the next fork in our chosen path. The expression "you take the high road or you take the low road" comes from this. Having this choice gives us the false belief that we do have control through our actions in how we live our lives. You might remember the famous poem from _Robert Frost (1874-1963)_, _"Two paths met in the woods, and I took the one less travelled, and it made all the difference."_ But ultimately, every path we take will lead to Death. And this picture from Life to Death, with its infinite variations of pathways you may choose to take, represents your Fate. Somehow, Fate knows when you are going to die even when you don't.

Then going back to the person who was killed by an object falling out of the sky, Fate put that person exactly in that spot and at that precise moment. Nothing that person could have done, by choosing a different pathway, would have prevented it because all these pathway choices lead to the same terminal point of death. At least that person, while ignorant, was blissful in not knowing when. So how did this person live before

Fate chose him or her to die in such an unfortunate and seemingly random manner? Suppose this person had pathway choices to either go to university, or to drop out of school altogether, and this person chose to go to university and became a medical doctor and helped find a cure for cancer which alleviated much suffering and pain. And let's say the alternate path lead this person to be a criminal who then became a serial killer or ended up immensely rich as a drug lord, adding to the evil and suffering in the world. In either case, Fate ended this person's life with an object out of the sky and there was nothing this person could have done to prevent it. And in the big picture, meaning our existence in context with our miniscule impact to the Universe, does it really matter whether that person lead a good or bad life? At the end, we are dead and the good or bad things we have done during our lives are only temporary as they will have no true long-term or everlasting effect. However, it does matter if we want to attain happiness in our lives. We know that good deeds will alleviate the suffering around us. We have all experienced suffering first-hand and we know that happiness cannot exist when there is suffering.

SCIENCE AND THE UNIVERSE

S cience has provided us with knowledge about the universe, matter, energy, gravity, space and time. All these things make up the world as we know it. But the more we learn and discover, the more we don't know and question. We cannot grasp the concept of infinity and how this would have any impact to our lives. We do not know what it really means to "live forever". What is forever? Do we want to live the way we are forever – slowly ageing and decaying with time? Is this the way we see eternal life? They say that our Universe started from the Big Bang, essentially from nothingness and our swirling galaxies are expanding into this vast emptiness of space and dark matter and energy, this seemingly infinite void of nothingness. Our day-to-day existence seems chaotic, but when you look at pictures of our Universe, you can see structure and order and immense beauty. Life cycles do exist in our Universe. They have always been there. Suns will be born, live and die, burning out in fiery explosions. Planets will be created and eventually expire or disappear into black holes. Our Universe will continue to expand to the point where it will stop expanding, and then all the galaxies will start collapsing back again into a single point of nothingness, waiting for the next big bang to occur. And this cycle will continue forever.

The Universe is limitless in size and scope, both at the microscopic and macroscopic levels. Because it is constantly changing, any conclusions drawn from currently accepted scientific knowledge and thoughts can be rendered lacking or meaningless. It is indeed very difficult to grasp the concept of infinite universes and infinite dimensions and realities. When you look into a single drop of water at the microscopic level, you can see whole new worlds of strange organisms, living and thriving totally oblivious of you. And when you go deeper into infinite smallness at the sub-atomic levels associated with the principles of quantum mechanics, there will no doubt exist other microscopic worlds and other dimensions beyond what we know to be our 3rd dimension which we live in. On a macro level, think of our universe with all its galaxies, stars and planets being contained in this same drop of water. Then consider this drop of water is part of vast oceans consisting of other similar drops each containing their own galaxies and worlds, just like our own. And these oceans are contained in another drop of water in other oceans in another universe or dimension, and so on. It becomes mentally impossible to visualize what infinity is. No doubt many religions in our world were created to try to explain the working of the Universe in terms that we might understand, so that we may be comforted that there must be both a reason and purpose for our existence.

Time and the Universe are synonymous with each other. Science has shown that time can be warped by gravity and that time travel to other dimensions or realities through portals in time is a possibility. Time is infinite, where past, present and future events are looped integrally, like a circle with no end. This means that **anything is possible with infinite time**. What we do in our lives and the physical things we leave behind as a legacy of our very short existence have absolutely no impact on the Universe. Given enough time, our vast cities and civilization will crumble back to dust and the life cycles can start anew. Humanity's average lifespan of 100 years is insignificant when it is compared with cosmic time of say, 500 billion years, if we can even imagine such a long timespan like this. We see remnants of dinosaurs 70 million years ago, but we don't know what existed on earth 700 million years ago. There is evidence of water on Mars, so 700 million years ago, could there have been life on Mars with civilizations far more advanced than ours? Might there be people like us in other planets in the Universe? Yes to both questions. Infinite time with the ever-changing Universe makes all this possible. The movie Star Wars came up with the concept of "the Force", whereby all living things, when they die, go back to this continuum of energy and matter making up the Universe. But this is somewhat limiting to include just living things, as all non-living things like rocks are made up of the same energy matter. And with infinite time, anything can evolve to anything else. And rocks one day can become alive.

With infinite time, reincarnation is possible and we can become anything in the Universe. I could become a strange plant-like creature in a distant planet, or a micro-organism living in a barren asteroid, or be re-incarnated as a powerful dictator somewhere in a future Earth, or be a god-like entity to a lower life forms in another galaxy. I can revert back to nothingness and become that rock and then be reborn again to be another rock, maybe bigger. When you venture beyond the limits to our existence as we know it, the possibilities are indeed endless. This is a wondrous world we live in, full of un-imaginable possibilities, for however long we are alive. Be comforted that the world we live in has structure and it has order. There has to be a reason why the Universe is as it is. The intelligence for such creation could not have come from nothingness. There is a purpose for it all – although that may forever remain a mystery to us. This mystery is our Life.

WHAT IS AN ABSOLUTE TRUTH?

People's beliefs are based on their personal values, perceptions, education and life experiences. What they believe to be true need not be either rational or even reasonable. Their beliefs make them who they are. Their truths may not be your truths. But different perspectives do not mean that only one interpretation of the truth is the correct one. Truths can become meaningless as continual change with time can alter the truths accepted today to be something totally different or false in the future. So, one may ask, "Is there an absolute truth?" – one that everyone can agree with regardless of their differences in life values, beliefs and cultural backgrounds? Yes, here are some examples of what may be considered to be absolute truths:

1. Our existence, in whatever form it is, will continue to change with time as nothing is constant or static. The Universe continues to evolve indefinitely.

2. The Universe was created by something - which can be a God, the Force, nature or science, or whatever you choose to call it.

3. The observable Universe has order and structure and beauty. It could not have been created randomly from chaos and nothingness.

4. Life and Death are intertwined and they are absolute truths. Death is the ending of Life, but it is not the end of everything.

Being open to the various perspectives and beliefs held by others will widen our understanding and appreciation of why things are the way they are in our own lives.

RELIGION AND LIFE

This uncertainty of what happens to us after death is probably the biggest reason why there are so many religious beliefs in the world. There must be a god, or something like a supreme entity or force that created the Universe and put the rules in place for its existence. People need to be comforted that their lives do account for something, and that there is a purpose for our existence ... that there is something more meaningful for us beyond death. But consider that religion is man-made and the prophets and spiritual leaders who started their religions were mere mortals who had gained wisdom contemplating the workings of the world, the reasons for their own existence and the meaning of Life and Death. They shared their wisdom and knowledge through their religions. From their years of meditation, they found this inner peace to accept Life for what it is. Simply, **we exist because we do, and that our existence will continue in some unknown form even after our death**. We cannot control this time we are alive. It will be whatever it will be.

113

The religions in the world would say that it does matter that people lead a good life – by having good morals and ethical values, filled with compassion, love and caring for each other and by being trustworthy, tolerant, supportive and kind. There are many "rules" to be followed if one is to expected to attain a "good" everlasting life after death. However, the concepts of good and evil, heaven and hell, nirvana or Valhalla, salvation and resurrection after death are all man-made to try to get people to do good during their lives so that they can be assured of a better life after death. These are noble goals to pursue in our very limited lifespan. But that hasn't stopped the hatred, killings, bigotry, envy and greed in the world. Humans have the capacity to be ruthless, violent and cruel. We will subjugate others, taking by force whatever we want, and killing without conscience or for just the sheer pleasure of it. Throughout history, this has been the nature of humankind. While we have the capacity for compassion and love, there still will be those who will choose the path of power, corruption, selfishness and hatred. But this choice of what we do with our lives is ours to make, especially when we have the free will to choose to do better.

LAWS OF NATURE

Human beings are different from the other animals. We have superior intellects and the ability to reason. We are capable of changing our environment. We are capable of immense compassion and love. We have a conscience and as sentient beings, we have an awareness and inquisitiveness of our surroundings. We have the free will to make choices. Animals are governed by the laws of nature and the survival of the fittest. Their purpose in life is to live, to pro-create and multiply, and to survive. They will kill other animals because they need to eat. They do not kill for the pleasure of it. And when animals and plants get eaten, there is no regret shown by the survivors. They just accept that this is life and it goes on. They are satisfied when they are well-fed, healthy and secure in their surroundings. They feel alive. The strongest animals will be the dominant ones and they will fight others within their own kind to maintain that status. They will fight with other species to defend themselves and their territories to ensure their survival. You can see the behavioural parallels shown by animals when men seek power and control over others in our own history. Humans are still animals. While we have evolved to the upper echelon of the animal hierarchy, we are still governed by the laws of nature. With infinite time, who can say what humankind might evolve to become.

OUR WORLD OF OPPOSITES

We live in a world of opposites - a world full of contradictions. In history, Chinese philosophy has recognized this phenomenon as "Yin – the negative, dark and feminine side" and "Yang – the positive, bright and masculine side" – opposites which govern the way we are and what we do. Men and women are opposites, yet we need each other to be complete and to survive. While opposites are supposed to be completely different, they are essentially the same. And opposites attract and they need each other to be complete. Just like magnets with opposite negative and positive poles. Just like men and women. They will attract and bond together as this will be the natural thing to do. This is evident in our world and Universe. Hot and cold are opposites, but extreme heat and extreme cold feels the same. They both hurt! Extreme love and extreme hatred can also feel similar and they have the same overpowering emotional effect. Pain and pleasure are opposites and they have been felt at the moment of our birth, at our beginnings of Life. There is tremendous pain and suffering at childbirth, followed by intense relief and joy when the baby is born. Women know this to be true. Men will never know the pain of childbirth. However, think of the time you had a severe leg cramp and the excruciating pain would not go away and you wished that you could die to get relief from the pain.

Then when the pain finally subsides, the relief is so intense that it is almost pleasurable. And of course, good and evil are opposites and you can see contradictions in our religions where good deeds are preached. Yet if your god is not their god, or your beliefs are different than theirs, or your physical appearance and customs are different than theirs, then you are not like them. You are a heathen, a sinner or infidel, and you are evil and you must be converted to their religion or be destroyed. Most wars in our history have been caused by religious differences and intolerance.

Life is a contradiction. There have been many stories written about the inherent violent nature of humans and that we would continue to be self-destructive even if we lived in a world like Shangri-La where it would be peaceful and harmonious, free from strife and wars and where only good resides and our every needs and desires would be fulfilled. Humans would die or destroy themselves in such an idyllic world. Humans need conflict and struggles to survive, to feel alive in their lives. This irony is our nature. We cannot help ourselves. This would explain a lot in why we continue to be the way we are and do the things we know to be detrimental to our existence. Yet we also want to do good because it makes us feel good. And when we feel good, we are happy. **We continually search for happiness in our lives. We expect to find it and to be** happy all the time. We don't want to suffer needlessly. **This is our purpose in life.** But we take happiness for granted and quickly forget all the times we have had happy experiences. In our world of opposites, happiness comes with many incidents of unhappy events. That is Life. In order to recognize true happiness, we must have a calmness in our thinking, this inner peace, enabling us to accept that this world of ours is full of contradictions and that our happiness is what we make out of it. That our happiness is within our control.

THE MEANING OF IT ALL

So how does all this help in understanding the purpose of our life and whether there is any meaning to it? Does this explain the events of the poor little girl who was crushed to death in front of her mother's eyes? Why did she have to die? Well, it was her time. What did she do to deserve to die? She did nothing to deserve to die. She didn't live long enough to do anything good or bad. Life is just random. Life does not have to be fair. Did she enjoy life? Yes, as a child she did experience happiness despite her abrupt ending. Will her mother survive the loss of her child? Yes, when she realizes that there was nothing she could have done about it. **Life goes on.** But her grief and sadness will be as equally great as her love and affection for her daughter in our world of opposites. <u>So, what was the purpose of the little girl's life?</u> Simply to exist, and she did. She experienced Life and while doing so, she provided much happiness to her mother. And they shared happiness together. With that, her life had both purpose and meaning.

Buddhism is a religion which respects the beliefs and deities of other religions. It does not demand that your god be the only god to be followed by everyone. If your religion and your god, or any beliefs you hold to be true, give you the peace of mind and the structure you need to survive and to make sense of the world you live in, then that is good as you will be happy. The _Dalai Lama (1935-present)_ got it right when he said that a common goal in life for every individual _"was to seek happiness and to be happy."_ And happiness means many different things to each of us and to all living things. But the key for a better world for us is **when you try to attain your happiness, in whatever form it is to you, do it not at the expense of the happiness of others**. It is quite a simple doctrine which is reflected in many religions. For example in Christianity, _"Do unto others as you would like done to yourself."_ But recognize that even if you follow a path towards a caring and compassionate life, this doesn't mean that everyone will do the same. Ironically in our world of opposites, for all the good we do and try to be, there will always be evil people doing

119

the opposite. That's the way things have been and will continue to be, at least in our lifetime. But we will always have the choice to try to do better and to try to be a good person. When we try to be our best, our lives and those around us can only be better and happier. Then **our lives can have both purpose and meaning when we create and share happiness with others**.

I do not fear the day when I am to die as it will happen when it is my time. Only then will I find out what exists beyond Death and whether these thoughts of mine are any closer to the true meaning of Life. Too bad we all have to die to find out the truth. But then again, maybe Death is the best thing that can happen to us in Life! There is no use in fearing or worrying about the unknown or what will become of us when we die. This is part of our acceptance that Life leads to Death. Simply live it, experience it. Try to live a good and honourable life as when you get older and contemplate what you have done in your lifetime, you can enjoy it again and be happy that you have lived and made a difference for those who knew you. Embrace Life for whatever time we have as Death will always be there, waiting for us. Acceptance will be easy when you find the inner peace to realize that this is the way things are and will continue to be. Spend some time alone, out in the darkness with the stars, without any external distractions, to think about your own mortality and wonder what this Life and Death are all about. Then you may see that the Universe has unfolded in exactly the way it should.

Being able to age and to live a long time is a gift in Life that should not be taken for granted. It means that you have experienced more of the things in life that are important to you. I remember my grandfather, _Willie Yep (1890-1974),_ saying at his death bed, _"I have lived a long life. My life has been good and I have no regrets for how I lived. I have seen all the things I needed to see in my life. I have been happy. I am ready to go."_ No fear. Just the acceptance of the inevitable as this was the natural progression of our journey from Life to Death. Death is not the end of Life, just a continuation of our existence, whatever it may be.

I leave with you some words which describe Life and Death so simply and poetically beautiful. These words came from _Chief Crowfoot (1830-1890)_ when he was facing his own mortality. I call it:

The Illusion of Life

A little while and I will be gone from among you
When, I cannot tell.
From nowhere we came.
Into nowhere we go.
What is Life?
It is the flash of a firefly in the night.

121

It is the breath of a buffalo in the wintertime.
It is the little shadow which runs across the grass
And loses itself in the sunset.

Life is an illusion, filled with opposites and random events. It can be short and fickle, harsh and cruel. Yet Life can also be filled with happiness and wonderful experiences. It is a matter of your own frame of mind. Accept that your life is exactly where it should be and that it will always be your choice as to what you want to do with it. **We exist because we received this gift called Life.** The intelligence that created Life also created Death. There is a purpose to our life which we may only discover when it is our time to go. Isn't Life so maddingly mysterious and wonderful?

SECTION III

WORDS of WISDOM (WOW)
QUOTATIONS for LIVING LIFE

CATEGORIES

This Section on quotations is divided into five categories. All quotes reflect some truth in Life that we have experienced. These quotes may be philosophical and profound, offering sage insights on how to live a good life, or be downright whimsical and silly, showing how capricious Life can be.

The quotations marked with an asterisk (*) have been referenced in the two previous sections.

The five categories are:

1. WOW – **QUOTES FOR LIFE**
2. WOW – **LESSONS IN LIFE**
3. WOW – **BUSINESS LESSONS**
4. WOW – **PROVERBS FOR LIFE**
5. WOW – **QUOTES TO REMEMBER**

What are your favourite quotes that reflect who you are? Hopefully, you will find a few in this section!

QUOTES FOR LIFE

Alfred d'Sousa
For a long time, it had seemed to me that life was about to begin - real life. But there was always some obstacle in the way, something to be got through first, some unfinished business, time still to be served, a debt to be paid. Then life would begin. At last, it dawned on me that these obstacles were my life.

Anonymous
We are not human beings having a spiritual experience in the universe. We are spiritual beings having a human experience.

Aristotle
What should we do to live a good life? Man can only achieve happiness by using all his abilities and capacities.

Carl Sagan *
A Universe with no edge in space, no beginning or end in time, and nothing for a Creator to do.

Chuang Tzu *
Once I dreamed I was a butterfly, and now I am no longer know whether I am I, who dreamed I was a butterfly, or whether I am a butterfly, dreaming that I am I.

Confucius
I sought for happiness and happiness eluded me. I turned to service and happiness found me.

Einstein *
The religion of the future will be a cosmic religion. It should transcend a personal god and avoid dogmas and theology. Covering both natural and spiritual, it should be based on a religious sense arising from the experience of all things, natural and spiritual and a meaningful unity.

Epicurus *
Is God willing to prevent evil, but not able? Then he is not omnipotent. Is he able, but not willing? Then he is malevolent. Is he both able and willing? Then whence cometh evil? Is he neither able nor willing? Then why call him God?

Epicurus *

Death is nothing to us, since when we are, death has not come, and when death has come, we are not.

Gandhi

One can find the deeper roots of one's own religion by looking at other religions, and then returning to see one's own faith with new eyes.

Harlan Edison *

For a brief time, I was here. And for a brief time, I mattered.

Jean-Paul Sartre *

It is imperative that Life must have meaning. But it is ourselves who must create this meaning in our own lives. To exist is to create your own life.

John Lennon

When I was 5 years old, my mother always told me that happiness was the key to life. When I went to school, they asked me what I wanted to be when I grew up. I wrote down "happy". They told me I didn't understand the assignment, and I told them they didn't understand life.

Joseph McInnes
The larger the island of knowledge, the longer the shoreline of wonder.

Jostein Gaarder *
If God created the Universe, then who created God?

Jostein Gaarder
The big philosophical questions: "Whether man has an eternal soul, whether there is a God, whether nature is immutable, and whether the universe is finite or infinite?"

Jostein Gaarder
We are the stuff such as dreams are made on, and our little life is rounded with sleep. [Is Life an illusion?]

J.R. Tolkein *
On Death: The gift of the One to Man, it is bitter to receive. Death is truly God's gift. Death is one unknown, a new, unexpected discovery. The loss and the silence of Death - it is our curse, but also our blessing.

Kierkegaard
Life can only be understood backwards, but must be lived forward.

Niels Bohr *

There are two kinds of truths. There are the superficial truths, the opposite of which are obviously wrong. But there are also the profound truths, those whose opposites are equally right.

Novalis *

The world becomes a dream, and the dream becomes reality.

Rene Descartes *

How can you be certain that your whole life is not a dream?

Richard Feynman *

I wonder why, I wonder why, I wonder why I wonder? I wonder WHY I wonder why, I WONDER WHY I WONDER!!

Robert Frost

In three words, I can sum up everything I've learned about Life. It goes on ...

Samuel Coleridge *

What if you slept? And what if, in your sleep, you dreamed? And what if, in your dream, you went to heaven and there plucked a strange and beautiful flower? And what if, when you awoke, you had the flower in your hand? Ah, what then?

Shakespeare *
Macbeth: "Life is but a walking shadow, a poor player that struts and frets his hour upon the stage and then is heard no more: it is a tale told by an idiot, full of sound and fury, signifying nothing."

Shakespeare *
What's done cannot be undone.

Socrates *
One thing only I know, and that is I know nothing.

Steve Jobs
Death is very likely the single best invention of Life. It is Life's change agent. It clears out the old to make way for the new. Right now, the new is you, but someday not too long from now, you will gradually become the old and be cleared away.

Tom Peters
On Life:" You do some stuff. Some works. You do more of what works. You do some more stuff. What works is copied by others. You do some more stuff."

Unknown
Purpose is what gives life meaning.

LESSONS IN LIFE

Albert Einstein
Out of clutter, find simplicity. From discord, find harmony. In the middle of difficulty lies opportunity.

Alexandre Dumas
Do not value money for any more or less than it is worth. It is a good servant, but a bad master.

Ally Condie
Nothing is really lost as long as you remember it.

Anonymous
If you are depressed, you are living in the past. If you are anxious, you are living in the future. If you are at peace, you are living in the moment.

Words of Wisdom
LESSONS IN LIFE

Anonymous
A man and a woman are like a pair of scissors. One blade is useless without the other.

Anonymous
There are some who complain about the thorns on roses. Other thank God for putting roses among the thorns.

Basil S. Walsh
If you don't know where you are going, how can you expect to get there.

Bob Talbert
Teaching kids to count is fine, but teaching them what counts is best.

Bobby McFerrin
Don't worry, be happy. (30 years old quote)

Buddha *
If one wishes to avoid certain types of results, one needs to change the conditions that give rise to them. This includes changing the condition of one's own state of mind.

C.S. Lewis
You can't go back and change the beginning, but you can start where you are and change the ending.

Charles Daniels
Money can change people's minds about most things.

Christie Blanchford
Truth always, no matter the consequences.

Clint Eastwood
If you can live your life and try to do as well as you can for your community and be helpful and do the best work you can, be the best mate or parent you can, then that's the best you can do.

Confucius
Our greatest glory is not in never falling, but rising every time we fall.

Dalai Lama *
Live a good and honourable life. Then when you get older and think back, you'll be able to enjoy it a second time.

Dalai Lama
Share your knowledge. It is a way to achieve
immortality.

Dalai Lama
Remember that not getting what you want is
sometimes a wonderful stroke of luck!

Dalai Lama
Why be unhappy about something if it can be
remedied? And what is the use of being unhappy if
it cannot be remedied? [A translation of Shantdeva's
famous question.]

Dalai Lama
Acceptance is the opposite of resignation and
defeat. Acceptance allows us to engage with life on
its own terms rather than rail against the fact that
life is not as we would wish. Stress and anxiety
come from our expectations of how life should be.
When we are able to accept that life is how it is, not
as we think it should be, then we can see the path to
our happiness.

David Suzuki's Father
You are what you do, not what you say.

Deepak Chopra *
Law of Acceptance: I know that this moment is as it should be, because the Universe has unfolded exactly in the way it should be.

Don Stanford
Experience is what you get when you don't get what you want.

Epicurus *
The gods are not to be feared. Death is nothing to worry about. Good is easy to attain. The fearful is easy to endure.

Ernest Hemingway
Worry a little bit every day and in a life-time you will lose a couple of years. If something is wrong, fix it if you can. But train yourself not to worry. Worry never fixes anything.

Fraser Allison
You die if you worry and you die if you don't, so why worry.

Friedrich Nietzsche
He who has a WHY to live for, can endure with almost any HOW.

Garth Brooks
You aren't really wealthy until you have something money can't buy. [Money can't buy integrity.]

George Burns
I'd rather be a failure at something I enjoy than to be a success at something I hate.

George Eliot
It is never too late to be what you might have been.

Goethe
He who cannot draw on three thousand years is living from hand to mouth.

Greg Clark
Ethics (integrity) is what you do when no one is looking.

Helen Keller
Security is mostly a superstition. It does not exist in nature, nor do the children of men as a whole experience it. Avoiding danger is no safer in the long run than outright exposure. Life is either a daring adventure or nothing.

Henry Ford
An airplane flies best against the wind. Translation: You need obstacles in your life to bring the best out of you!

Hugh Jackman
Movie: The Greatest Showman - "Every one of us is special and no one is like anyone else."

Hunter S. Thompson
Who is the happier man? He who has braved the storm of life and lived, or he who has stayed securely on shore and merely existed?

J.C. Watts
Character is doing the right thing when no one is watching.

J.K. Rowland
Failure gave me an inner security that I had never attained by passing examinations. Failure taught me things about myself that I could have learned no other way.

James D. Miles
You can easily judge the character of a man by how he treats those who can do nothing for him.

Jennifer Lopez
You make a mistake and you think why there isn't anything good in your life. The truth is that these mistakes sometimes lead you to exactly where you are supposed to be, to what you're supposed to learn, to get you to your actual real happy place.

Jet Li
A follower of Tibetan Buddhism: "If I learn how to die, I will understand how to enjoy life. And that will enable me to show a good heart to the world."

John Wooden
It's what you learn after you know it all that counts.

Judge Judy Sheindlin
The easiest thing in the world is to tell the truth, then you don't have to remember what you said.

Ken Blanchard
People with humility don't think less of themselves, they just think of themselves less.

La Donna Harris
Wealth is something you acquire so you can share it, not keep it.

Leonard Cohen *
Everyone knows ... that the dice are loaded ... that the war is over and the good guys lost ... that the boat is leaking and the captain lied ... that the fight was fixed, and the poor stay poor and the rich get rich ...

Life's Golden Rules
Learn the art of schmoozing, but don't make it your greatest talent.

Life's Golden Rules
Think a conflict through from the other person's point of view.

Lord Acton *
Power corrupts. Absolute power corrupts absolutely.

Marcel Proust
The voyage in discovery lies not in finding new landscapes, but in having new eyes.

Margaret Fuller
If you have the knowledge, let others light their candles by it.

Words of Wisdom
LESSONS IN LIFE

Mark Twain
The two most important days in your life are the day
you were born and the day you find out why.

Maya Angelou
Success is liking yourself, liking what you do, and
liking how you do it.

Mother Teresa
Kind words can be short and easy to speak, but their
echoes are truly endless.

Mother Teresa
If you judge people, you have no time to love them.

Nelson Mandela
Education is the most powerful weapon which you
can use to change the world.

Olin Miller
We probably wouldn't worry what other people
thought of us if we knew how seldom they do.

Oscar Wilde
Experience is simply the name we give our mistakes.

Pablo Picasso
Only put off until tomorrow what you are willing to
die having left undone.

Pope Francis
Better to be an atheist than a hypocrite.

Robert E. Lee
Good judgment comes from experience. And
experience comes from bad judgment.

Robert Frost *
Two roads diverged in the woods, and I took the one
less traveled by, and that has made all the
difference.

Roger C. Anderson
Accept that some days you're the pigeon, and some
days you're the statue.

Sandra Carey
Never mistake knowledge for wisdom. One helps
you make a living; the other helps you make
a life.

Sheri Madigan

Generosity is defined as the quality of being kind and giving time, attention or gifts to others without conditions or the expectation of getting something in return. Being generous is seen as a positive virtue in people and it has links with other emotions such as empathy and compassion.

Sigmund Freud

Unfortunately, repressed emotions do not die. They are silenced, but they continue to affect the person.

Simone de Beauvoir *

In our culture, women are treated as the second sex. Men behave as if they are the subjects, treating women like their objects, thus depriving them of the responsibility of their own life.

Sir Isaac Newton *

His third law of physics applies to ordinary day-to-day life: "For every action, there will be an equal and opposite reaction", or simply said, there are consequences for your actions.

Sir Winston Churchill

The greatest lesson in life is to learn that even fools are right sometimes.

Socrates
He who knows what is good, will do good.

Sophocles
Rather fail with honor than succeed by fraud.

Stephen Hawking *
The greatest enemy of knowledge is not ignorance,
it is the illusion of knowledge.

Stephen Hawking
Be curious. And however difficult life may seem,
there is always something you can do and succeed
at. It matters that you don't just give up.

Thomas Szasz
Knowledge is gained by learning; trust by doubting;
skill by practising; and love by loving.

Tony Yep
Sometimes, the best you can do is not good enough.
But it is the best you can do and you tried.

Tony Yep
To get trust, you must first give trust.

Words of Wisdom
LESSONS IN LIFE

Tony Yep
With honesty comes integrity.

Unknown
Do not regret growing old. It is a privilege denied to many.

Unknown
What is, simply is. Allow it and rejoice in it.

Unknown
Conscience is like the demarcation on the highway. It tells us what we shouldn't do, but it can't stop us from doing it.

Unknown
Choice, not chance, determines one's destiny.

Shakespeare
No legacy is as rich as honesty.

WISDOM
The more sand that has escaped from the hourglass of our life, the clearer we should see through it.

BUSINESS LESSONS

Abraham Lincoln
Nearly all men can stand adversity, but if you want to test a man's character, give him power.

Abraham Maslow
If the only tool you have is a hammer, it is tempting to treat everything as if it were a nail.

Andrew Carnegie
As I grow older, I pay less attention to what men say. I just watch what they do.

Aristotle *
He who is a good ruler must first have been ruled.

Baron de Rothschild
Making money doesn't oblige people to forfeit their honor or their conscience.

Brian Mulroney

On Winston Churchill: Leadership is not something learned in school. It is innate, an indelible mark of character steeped in integrity, courage, conviction, underscored by the moral imperative to do the right thing.

Don Braid

Once lost, trust is difficult to regain.

George Santayana

Those who cannot learn from history are doomed to repeat it.

Greg Thompson

No one cares what you think until they think you care.

Henry Ford

You can't build a reputation on what you are going to do.

James Ling

Don't tell me how hard you work. Tell me how much you get done.

Jill Ruckelshaus
The best way to win an argument is to begin by being right.

Jim Collins
People are not the most important asset. The right people are.

Jimmy Durante
Be nice to people on your way up because you will meet them on your way down.

Kevin Doherty
Investment dollars are like water as they will take the path of least resistance.

Kurt Lewis
If you want to truly understand something, try to change it.

Lance Murray
You can't make chicken salad out of chicken shit!

Lester B. Pearson
Diplomacy is letting someone else have their way.

Life's Golden Rules
The best leader is not the one who makes the fewest mistakes, but the one who makes the best of them.

Life's Golden Rules
Taking the time to do it right beats taking the time to do it over.

Life's Golden Rules
Incompetence knows no barriers of time or place. It is found everywhere.

Life's Golden Rules
Time lost is retrievable. Time wasted is eternal

Lou Holtz
I never learn anything talking. I only learn things when I ask questions.

Michael Crichton
If it's consensus, it isn't science. If it's science, it isn't consensus.

MISTAKES
It could be that the purpose of your life is only to serve as a warning to others!

Murphy's Law Extra

When things are going well, something will go wrong as you will have overlooked something. When things just can't get any worse, they will.

Occan's Razor

All things being equal, the simplest explanation is usually the correct one. This underpins virtually every scientific discovery ever made. In politics, it is often incompetence, rather than scruples, that makes the simplest explanation most likely.

Peter Drucker

Management is doing things right. Leadership is doing the right things.

Peter Drucker

The most important thing in communication is to hear what isn't being said.

Peter Principle

In a hierarchy, everyone tends to rise to his/her level of incompetence.

Ralph Waldo Emerson

The reward of a thing well done is to have done it.

Rudy Guiliani

To be a leader, you really have to care for people, to like them. If you are there for them, they will be there for you.

Sam Ewing

Nothing is so embarrassing as watching someone do something that you said couldn't be done.

Simon Sinek

People don't buy what you do: they buy why you do it.

Sir Richard Branson

You can't succeed in everything, but you can learn a lot in the process.

Spiderman / Stan Lee

With great power comes great responsibility.

Stephen Covey

The 7 Habits of Highly Effective People - "Seek first to understand, then to be understood." Improve understanding by paraphrasing.

Tony Yep

Recognize that there will be times you will need help as you can't do or know everything.

Tony Yep
The Law of Unintended Consequences: However noble the intention or the objective may be for the decision made, there may be un-intended consequences.

Unknown
In business, you can go far by doing what is right, and not just saying what is right.

Unknown
The best executive (manager) is the one who has sense enough to pick good people to do what he wants done, and the self-restraint enough to keep from meddling with them while they do it.

Unknown
A compromise is an agreement whereby both parties get what neither of them wanted.

Unknown
As long as you want to have power over others, you cannot fully trust them.

Unknown
The man who wants to be great should be an honest man first.

Unknown
Look after your people and treat them well, and in return, they will be loyal and hardworking.

Unknown
Choice, not chance, determines destiny. But sometimes it is good to be lucky.

Unknown
Motivation is what gets you started. Habit is what keeps you going.

Vince Lombardi
If it doesn't matter who wins or loses, why bother keeping score?

PROVERBS FOR LIFE

Aesop
It is easy to be brave from a safe distance.

Albert Yep *
When it is time for you to go, it's time for you to go.

American Proverb
Before borrowing money from a friend, decide which you need the most.

Anonymous
Give a man a truth and he will think for a day. Teach a man to reason and he will think for a lifetime.

Bryan Gilbert
Wherever you go, there you are!

Buddhist Scripture

In each atom of the realms of the Universe, there exist vast oceans of world systems.

Chinese Proverb

In Cantonese "Lok yip quay gan" - The fallen leaves go back to the roots.

Confucius

Choose a job you love and you will never have to work a day in your life.

Dalai Lama *

In the pursuit of your happiness, try not to attain it at the expense of the happiness of others.

Dalai Lama *

On Enlightenment: Bringing order out of chaos, light out of darkness, day out of night and existence out of nothingness.

Democritus *

Nothing can come from nothing. Nothing can change, and nothing is ever lost.

English Proverb

A stumble may prevent a fall.

Friedrich Nietzsche

That which does not kill us, makes us stronger.

Gandhi

Be the change you want to see in the world.

Japanese Proverb

When the character of a man is not clear to you, look at his friends.

Lao Tzu

"Tao Te Ching": The journey of a thousand miles begins with a single step.

Mahatma Gandhi

The Seven Deadly Sins: Wealth without work, pleasure without conscience, knowledge without character, commerce without morality, science without humanity, worship without sacrifice and politics without principle.

Martin Luther King Jr.
The time is always right to do what is right.

Rene Descartes *
"Cognito, ergo sum": I think, therefore, I am.

Rumi *
We come whirling out of nothingness, scattering
stars like dust.

Unknown
Do not follow where the path may lead. Go instead
where there is no path and leave a trail.

William Wordsworth
That best portion of a good man's life, his little,
nameless, unremembered acts of kindness and love.

QUOTES TO REMEMBER

Abraham Lincoln
Whatever you are, be a good one.

Allen Funt
When people are smiling, they are most receptive to almost anything you want to teach them.

Anonymous
Knowledge is knowing a tomato is a fruit. Wisdom is not putting it in a fruit salad.

Anonymous
Why not learn to enjoy the little things. There are so many of them.

Anonymous
There are three kinds of people: those who can count, and those who can't! And then there are those who are clueless!

Anonymous
Theory is when you know everything, but nothing works. Practical is when everything works, but nobody knows why. When both theory and practical are combined, nothing works and nobody knows why!

Anonymous
Having it all doesn't mean having all it at once.

Anonymous
I used to be conceited. But now, I am just perfect!

Arnold H. Glasgow
A true friend never gets in your way unless you happen to be going down.

Barry Weiss
Bridge is a lot like sex. If you don't have a great partner, you'd better have a good hand!

Barry Wilken
A retiree turning 65 or 70: Most days I do nothing, but it takes me all day to do it.

Ben Hogan
The most important shot in golf is the next one.

Buddha
Holding onto anger is like drinking poison and expecting the other person to die.

Deepak Chopra
All activity in nature is silent. Completely silent. And it involves the principle of least effort. Do less, accomplish more. Ultimately, do nothing and you will accomplish everything.

Derek Bok
If you think education is expensive, try ignorance.

Dr. Joyce Brothers
The two hardest things to handle in life are failure and success.

Eleanor Roosevelt
Great minds discuss ideas, average minds discuss events, small minds discuss people.

Words of Wisdom
QUOTES TO REMEMBER

Eric Froman
If I am what I have and if I lose what I have, who then am I?

Erica Jong
Advice is what we ask for when we already know the answer, but wish we didn't.

Erin Majors
A candle loses nothing by lighting another candle.

Faye Flam
People are ignorant of their ignorance.

Fred Clark
It's hard to detect good luck - it looks so much like something you've earned.

Gary Snyder
True affluence is not needing anything.

George Brookman
Someone once said to me, 'Cheer up! Things could be worse.' So I cheered up and, sure enough, things got worse.

George Bernard Shaw
Take care to get what you like, or you will be forced to like what you get.

Giuseppe Tomasi
If you want things to stay as they are, things will have to change.

H. Jackson Brown
Success is getting what you want. Happiness is liking what you get.

Haim Ginott
Children are like wet cement. Whatever falls on them makes an impression.

James Allen
Work joyfully and peacefully, knowing that right thoughts and right efforts will inevitably bring about right results.

James Bond
From Casino Royale: "Why is it that people who can't take advice insist on giving it."

Jayson Feinburg

I wear my wife's eyeglasses because she wants me to see things her way.

Jean Chretien

Canadian Prime Minister: A proof is a proof, and when you have a good proof, it's because it's proven. Duh??

Jim Gehl

As long as people continue to see themselves as victims, they will never take responsibility for their actions. It is easy to be a victim, because you don't have to do anything. But in the long run, playing the victim [or race] card is self-defeating.

Johnny Carson

Talent alone won't make you a success. And neither will being in the right place at the right time unless you are ready.

Jordan Peterson

I do not believe in God, but I'm afraid He might exist.

Jostein Gaarder
Whatever survives is right, or that which is right survives.

Karl Marx *
Religion is the sigh of the oppressed creature …. the heart of a heartless world, and the soul of soul-less conditions. It is the opium of the people.

Ken S. Keyes Jr.
To be upset over what you don't have is to waste what you do have.

Leonardo da Vinci
Painting is poetry that is seen rather than felt, and poetry is painting that is felt rather than seen.

Life's Golden Rules
There is only one chance to make a good first impression.

Life's Golden Rules
Success is a journey, not a destination.

Life's Golden Rules
Asking stupid questions is your right - just don't abuse the privilege!

Life's Golden Rules
It is better to keep your mouth shut at the risk of people thinking you are dumb, than to open it and remove all doubt.

Malcolm Forbes
Being right half the time beats being half-right all the time!

Mohammad Ali
Float like a butterfly, sting like a bee!

Moliere
It infuriates me to be wrong when I know I'm right.

Norman MacEwan
We make a living by what we get, but we make a life by what we give.

Pamela Anderson
When someone doesn't think you are intelligent, then you form a full sentence, you are a genius!

Paul Dean
The nice thing about meditation is that it makes doing nothing quite respectable.

Picasso
When I was a child, my mother said to me, 'If you become a soldier, you'll be a general. If you become a monk, you'll end up as the pope.' Instead, I became a painter and wound up as a Picasso.

Picasso
A work of art must not be something that leaves a man unmoved, something he passes by with a casual glance. It has to make him react, feel strongly, start creating too, if only in his imagination.

Pierre Corneille
The manner in which it is given is worth more than the gift.

Plato
Only the understanding that comes from within can lead to true insight.

Words of Wisdom
QUOTES TO REMEMBER

Ralph Klein
When mayor of Calgary, speaking of rival city
Edmonton: "Edmonton is not the end of the world,
but you can see it from there!"

Richard Feynman
Science is a satisfactory philosophy of ignorance.

Robert Frost
The world is full of willing people, some willing to
work, the others willing to let them.

Roy McEvoy (Movie: Tin Cup)
Someone said that golf and sex are two things you
don't have to be good at to enjoy!

Sally Forth
Better to be alone than with someone you wish
were dead.

Socrates
A philosopher is one who loves wisdom. A
philosopher knows that in reality he knows very
little. That is why he constantly strives to achieve
true insight.

166

Words of Wisdom
QUOTES TO REMEMBER

Spock (Star Trek)
The needs of the many outweigh the needs of the few, or the one.

Stephen Hawking
If Stephen Hawking can't come up with a unified theory of the universe, then what chance for us mortals to understand it at all.

Stephen Hawking *
When asked what he thinks of most, "Women... they are a complete mystery."

Stephen Hawking *
Quantum theory of gravity - one that combines the general theory of relativity (gravity and the macro-universe) with quantum mechanics (atoms and the micro-universe) to result in a comprehensive unified theory of the universe.

The Rolling Stones
You can't always get what you want.

Thomas Jefferson
Honesty is the first chapter of the book of wisdom.

Words of Wisdom
QUOTES TO REMEMBER

Tony Robbins
If you do what you've always done, you'll get what you've always gotten.

Tony Yep
On Fate: My Father once told me that if it were meant for me to be rich, I would find a lotto ticket in the street, and it will be the winning number.

Tony Yep
We've all heard about: "Happy wife, happy life!" Here's one for the poor husband who is always taken for granted: "Happy hubby, life is bubbly!"

Tony Yep *
Be glad you are human and not a rock!

Unknown
If you haven't got all the things you want, be grateful for the things you don't have that you don't want.

Unknown
Kentucky Fried: I am the gaping void where Loneliness resides. The song in my heart turns mournful and off-key. Where have you gone? Where have you gone?

Unknown
Artificial Intelligence is no match for natural stupidity.

Unknown
An apology is a good way to have the last word.

Unknown
There is a first time and a last time for everything.

Unknown
What's right isn't always popular, and what's popular isn't always right.

Unknown
For those who talk too much: "Silent and listen are spelled with the same letters!"

Warren Buffet
No matter how great the talent or efforts, some things just take time. You can't produce a baby in one month by getting nine women pregnant.

Zoey Duncan
A hobby is done for pleasure, it requires some skill and it has a satisfying outcome.

RECOMMENDED READING

Dalai Lama – "The Universe in a Single Atom – The Convergence of Science and Spirituality"

Deepak Chopra – "The Seven Spiritual Laws of Success"

John Heider – "The Tao of Leadership"

Jostein Gaarder – "Sophie's World – A Novel about the History of Philosophy"

Lindsay Green – "You Could Live a Long Time: Are you Ready?"

Richard P. Feynman – "Surely You're Joking, Mr. Feynman"

Stephen W. Hawking – "A Brief History of Time – From the Big Bang to Black Holes"

Tony Yep – "Quality Management Works!" 1996 Project Management Institute (PMI) Symposium in Calgary. This article is about the differences between a democratic versus an autocratic management style. The concepts are still valid today. Available on the author's website: https://drygon.ca

INDEX OF BOOK

INDEX OF BOOK

INDEX OF BOOK

INDEX OF BOOK

INDEX OF QUOTATIONS

INDEX OF QUOTATIONS

INDEX OF QUOTATIONS

181

INDEX OF QUOTATIONS

INDEX OF QUOTATIONS

ABOUT THE AUTHOR

Tony Yep is a mechanical engineer by profession, having graduated from McGill University in 1971. He has had a very successful career as an engineering and project manager. His technical background forces him to look at all the facts objectively and logically, using proven scientific data and knowledge to determine what can be true, or reasonable, and possible.

It has taken him this long to gain the life experience and wisdom to be able to make sense of the issues of Life. It is hoped that some of the insights in this book will resonate with you. His own views on Life and Death have changed in writing this book.

Contact Info:
Website: https://drygon.ca   Email: tyep49@gmail.com

(

Made in the USA
Columbia, SC
06 October 2020

22166625R00113